Living Joyfully Free

By Lisa Buffaloe

~ *Dedication* ~

To Jesus Christ, my amazing Savior, thank You for Your grace, mercy, peace, and joy that blesses us with the ability in Living Joyfully Free!

~ *Come On Over* ~

Hi, I'm so glad you are here. Thank you for joining me. As you visually stroll through these pages, I've left devotions, ponderings, and contemplations to hopefully bring you closer to God.

This isn't a regular devotion book. Each page is a stepping stone, a place to pause and ponder, a field to run through, a mountain to climb, a river to splash and play in God's Living water. A picnic on the Bread of Life with The Bread of Life. Time along a garden pathway in the sun to be Son-kissed by God's Son. Come on over and let's explore living joyfully free with our wonderful God.

~ *Living Joyfully Free* ~

Where is the abundant life God promised in the midst of illness, suffering, or catastrophe? To be honest, it's often hard to find. Sometimes life just stinks. Life is hard and difficult. People do and say terrible things. You just have to go with the flow. Admit the truth. The waters get deep, the fires get hot, but God never leaves our side.

The more trials I have endured, the more I've experienced God's unending faithfulness and love. With each hurdle crossed, each skirmish survived, comes strength, fulfillment, and joy.

God calls to each of our hearts to not only have eternal life but live victorious lives. Living joyfully free in Christ is similar to falling back into someone's arms, releasing our worries, problems, concerns, and fears to the capable, mighty hands of God.

When our son was beginning to walk, he would latch onto something for support. If he held onto the coffee table, he stood on his feet and walked. If he held our hands, he walked. As long as something was connected to his hand, he believed he could walk, and he did.

Finally growing in confidence, he placed one hand on his shirt gripped it like crazy, and walked across the room. If he took his hand off his shirt, he crashed to the floor. Hand on shirt, he walked. He trusted and had confidence in his belief that what he held would give him support. His shirt was not his true source of support, and once he knew his legs would hold him up and he could walk on his own, he ran free.

What we know, believe, and trust makes us who we are. God wants us to run free, enjoying who we are in Christ. God wants the best for us, to bring the best to us, to bring the best out of us, to live the best life.

Trust that God wants more, and has much more planned for your future. God is a God of pressed down, shaken together, free-flowing, abundant life. Living joyfully free doesn't mean we won't have trouble or problems, but in allowing God to take full control—trusting and believing He has your best interest at heart.

Living joyfully free doesn't mean all is right with the world but knowing all is right with God.

Heavenly Father thank You that no matter how crazy this world is, and how wild my circumstances may be, I can live joyfully free knowing You love me and my future is safe in Your loving hands.

~ Sometimes Life Stinks ~

As a little girl, I loved fairy tales and exciting action stories. The good guy (or girl) has cool gadgets, incredible adventures, and always wins in the end. In those stories there is always a hardship or quest to overcome. The more the hero fought, the louder the cheers when he reached his goal. I wanted to live in the fairy tale world, because I led a secret life.

No one knew what happened outside my safe, Christian home—the molestation by a baby sitter, the attacks, the rape, the other incidents. Each instance was stuffed, and I refused to acknowledge the trauma to others or myself. I moved into adulthood and the difficulties continued with divorce, being stalked, sexually harassed at work, cervical cancer, the death of friends and loved ones, over eleven years of chronic illness due to Lyme Disease, numerous hospitalizations with a bevy of strange diagnosis, along with seven surgeries.

In 2006 while fighting Lyme Disease, I had been tethered to a 24/7 PICC-line delivering intravenous antibiotics directly to my heart for 137 days. A raging fever signaled a blood infection. Packed in ice packs from head to toe, I whimpered in bed as my tears turned into a full-fledged pity party. Hyperventilating and desperate, I speed-dialed a friend. She prayed and talked with me until I could compose myself.

Then, she told me basically that my life really stunk.

I broke out in laughter. Because I was used to Christian platitudes, verses, the pat on the arm with an off-the-cuff "I'll pray for you," even some judgmental people who said my faith must be too small or I would be healed. My friend's comment turned my pity party into a joy party. Because it's true, life at times does stink. No judgment, no platitudes, just the plain truth. Ah, so refreshing.

And the wonderful thing I've found is that even when horrible things happen, God's love never fails. There is no pain too deep, no life too stinky, for God's gentle, healing, restoring, redeeming touch.

Heavenly Father even when the enemy has covered us in the stink of his mess, Your love is stronger and Your power mightier. Thank You that nothing is too hard for You to redeem or restore.

~ Stink Bombs ~

We all have them, the collection of stink bombs—things the enemy has done to us or the messes we've created. They are nauseous and often downright embarrassing. The enemy bombards our minds and thoughts attempting to make us doubt God and His goodness. Or the enemy taunts that we aren't good enough, that God (or anyone else) won't love us after what we've been through or what we've done.

I've lived in the stink for years, hiding myself in the smoke screen trying to convince myself and everyone else that all was right with the world. But limping through life isn't what God intended. Jesus came to set the captives free. Not partially free, somewhat free, maybe a little free, but completely and totally free.

When the enemy throws stink bombs, God blows back the stink to restore, renew, and use everything for good. When we allow God to walk us through and provide soul healing, He uses our difficulties to help in the battle for others.

What better way to defeat the enemy than turning the evil used against us to provide freedom for others? All around us, people are dying – mentally, physically, and spiritually. And our stories may well be part of their rescue. What the enemy used to hurt you, throw back on him, heap the mess right back on his slimy head by allowing God to heal you and share your testimony.

Each week I am blessed to interview people for Living Joyfully Free Radio. Every person has a story, a testimony of God's faithfulness. Those who wallowed in the mud of sin, God picked them up, dusted them off, and set them on their feet again, granting unfailing, unmerited, grace, and favor. The list of the enemy's "stink bombs" are now mere markers of God's amazing healing and restoration.

God never fails to forgive sins. He never fails to heal the wounds of the past. He daily grants beauty through His wonderful creation. He supplies every need. And every day He lavishes His extravagant love.

God never fails us. Even on days when we wonder where He is and why our situation doesn't change, God never fails us. Even when we can't see what will happen next, God never fails.

And God will never fail you. Regardless of what messes the enemy has heaped on your head, God's extravagant love never fails.

God's love ... endures forever, is faithful, just, righteous, merciful, abounding in love, great, everlasting to everlasting, gracious, compassionate, slow to anger, rich, covenant of love, love that makes deserts bloom, love that reaches to the heavens, living water love, the love of Christ is wide, long, high, and deep, love that floods the soul with joy, unfailing love.

For the word of the Lord holds true, and we can trust everything he does. He loves whatever is just and good; the unfailing love of the Lord fills the earth. ~ Psalm 33:4-5 NLT

~ God Happened ~

When I was in high school my Dad found a small farmhouse on ten acres near where his new job was located. He purchased the land for $35,000 and then proudly showed the family. My mother sat on the front porch and cried.

The yard had been swept clean (literally), and the surrounding land was infested with ticks and snakes. The underbrush beyond the yard was so thick you could stand anywhere away from the house and not see two feet beyond -- yep, we owned the land as far as the eye could see.

The kitchen was painted Pepto Bismol pink with yellow and brown counter tile, the small laundry room was "Lydia Pinkum Gray" (scary, huh?), other rooms were painted blue and green.

There was no such thing as neutral in this house. There was only one tiny bathroom for our family of five. The closets were only large enough for Sunday clothes and a pair of overalls.

During our first month, my dad killed twelve poisonous snakes. Dad became so adept at snake removal the Blue-jays took notice. They literally flew to him, chirped to get his attention, then would lead him to where a snake was hiding. The slithering varmints didn't have a chance. The final tally before my parents moved – sixty three poisonous snakes.

Why did my Dad buy the home? It had beautiful "bones." Underneath the interesting paint choices and the tangle of shrubs, stood a beautiful home and land.

However, revealing its inner beauty was a long, hard process. Our family did the majority of the work—sanding and staining the hardwood floors, framing in and adding new closet spaces, along with paint, paint, and more paint.

During this process, the well ran dry, and we literally stood on the little stoop of a porch washing our hair in the rain. We brought in water from other sources for drinking and cleaning. With the new, deeper well came the blessings of clear, rust free water.

People driving by would slow down; some would stop, watching in amazement at the transformation of the little farmhouse.

God looks at our lives and sees the potential to conform us to the image of His son. He gently (sometimes painfully) scrapes away the old paint, clears out the underbrush, kills the snakes, digs deeply into His cool, clear, refreshing living water and creates something beautiful.

Those who pass by will marvel at the testimony of changed and restored lives.

And when they ask, "Wow, what happened to you?" We can tell them, God happened!

For we are God's masterpiece. He has created us anew in Christ Jesus, so we can do the good things he planned for us long ago. ~ Ephesians 2:10 NLT

~ *Focusing* ~

Often the things we see as negatives are really positives as they bring us closer to God's heart. When we understand that God's love is for us, and tailor-made, and not against us, it becomes a cornerstone. Abundant living is not just about life, it's about living in Christ, finding who we are in Him.

Even though God has been with me every step of the way, sometimes I thought He had left, and several times I hoped He *wasn't* watching or listening.

Not everyone will undergo rough circumstances and thank goodness there is only one book of Job. However, we all will have our trials, some big and some small. Some people seem to have easier lives than others. God's purposes are beyond anything we can imagine. God really has been working in me and hammering home the point that He is all I need and will provide all I need.

Living beyond our circumstances comes from making the choice to focus on God, keeping our eyes on Him, and not on the bumpy road behind or ahead.

If you would be willing, please hold up your hand in front of your eyes. What do you see?

You see your hand.

In the same way when we focus on our problems, our view of God is obscured.

However when we zoom in our spiritual vision, and focus on the vastness, might, and power of our infinite God, our difficulties are brought into perspective that nothing is too hard for our God.

Heavenly Father help me always remember that nothing is impossible for You. There is no problem, no situation, no person, and no difficulty too big for You. Keep my focus on You and Your might, strength, power, and love.

~ God's Ointment ~

Two unfriendly looking spots were surgically removed from my back and shoulders. One area was deep enough to require both internal and external stitches. Thankfully, all biopsies came back fine.

However, the deepest area wouldn't heal and remained red and tender to the touch. During the day I could ignore the problem, but getting comfortable at night was quite a predicament.

While preparing the ointment and Band-Aids, I happened to glance at the antibiotic cream's expiration date. Oh my goodness, the date was **LONG** past overdue. Argh! No wonder I wasn't healing.

I have places in my heart that seem to take far too long to heal. Unfortunately I also have a tendency to overlook issues until all is quiet, then insecurities and memories cause an uncomfortable restlessness.

Ignoring problems are only band-aid fixes. Covering them with self-made medications, or feigning self-ignorance, doesn't work any better than long expired antibiotics.

God is the Great Physician. He repairs heartaches, the damages brought by our own sin or the sin of others, and hidden hurts from someone else's mean or careless actions or remarks.

If I keep applying expired medications, my sore won't heal. And if I keep trying to handle things my own way, with my own ineffective methods, my soul won't get well. So I'm throwing out the bad meds and applying the ointment of God's truth and healing for both body and soul.

No external or internal wound is too deep for God's healing touch. So remember to follow God's direction and daily apply God's word.

Heal me, O LORD, and I will be healed; Save me and I will be saved, for You are my praise. ~ Jeremiah 17:14 NASB

~ *Pass The Past* ~

Satan loves to dig up old bones, especially ugly, dirty, bad bones. The grungy bony sins we committed or others committed against us. A veritable bone yard of past issues, bad memories, and tormenting nightmares. The enemy digs them up or hands us a shovel and points to where they are buried.

We all have our yesterdays – The Past. Bad events. Bad mistakes. Bad memories. Unfulfilled dreams. Unfulfilled longings. The should have beens, the should have saids, the shouldn't haves, play and replay.

We circle around and around, dissecting, exploring, wondering, agonizing, and focusing on past events.

If the past keeps coming back to acknowledge unconfessed sin, hand that old bone to God and let His freedom, forgiveness, and healing wash you clean. Otherwise, when the past resurfaces, move on past with the promises and truth in God's word.

With God's help we can move into the new now. We can move forward into the future with hope. Because we know in all things God works for the good of those who love Him, who have been called according to His purpose.

Nothing is impossible with God.

Through God and the mercy and resurrection of Jesus Christ, He has given us new birth into living hope. So we can put on the new self, created to be like God in true righteousness and holiness, even made new in the attitude of our minds.

Our new self is being renewed in knowledge in the image of our Creator.

In Christ, we are a new creation; the old has gone, the new has come! It is by God's great mercy that we have been born again. So we can live with great expectation, knowing we have a priceless inheritance—an inheritance kept in heaven, pure and undefiled, beyond the reach of change and decay. ~ Romans 8:28, Luke 1:37, 2 Corinthians 5:17, Ephesians 4:23-24, Colossians 3:10, 1 Peter 1:3-4.

Heavenly Father, help me to stop circling the past or viewing the old bones. What You have forgiven is gone, and the past is past. Thank You that in Christ, I am a new creation with a new future!

~ Soul-Deep ~

We need to know and believe – Soul deep believing – that God loves us. Most of us can quote John 3:16. We know that God loved the world so much that He gave His one and only Son that when we believe in Him we have eternal life. Quoting Bible verses is easy; believing is harder, and even harder to live like we say we believe. Without the proper focus, we are half-hearted, weak, ineffective, unfocused, worried, fearful, and held captive by a defeated foe.

Do we really believe God loves us?

Within each of us is a longing for a grand love affair—something that makes us alive and filled to the brim—a true life fairy tale where the prince rescues and takes us to happily-ever-after land.

The wonderful thing is, there really is a happy-ever-after. We have a God who is our King and rescuer. Heaven offers the final rescue we innately crave. But here's the better news: even now, every need, every desire, every hollow place of our soul can be filled by God.

John 10:10 states that Jesus came to give us abundant life, and abundant isn't stagnant, it is life overflowing. Through Christ we reestablish the divine connection severed by sin. And divine connections are not ordinary. Divine connections are dynamic, growing, and vibrant.

God is a God of pressed down, shaken together, and running over. God blesses with life, and even better than that He blesses through Christ a guaranteed happy ending. Where else can you find a love that is unfailing, pure, and eternal?

Don't forget … Regardless of how other people treat you, see you, or don't see you. Regardless of how you feel. Regardless of your circumstances. Regardless of where you've been, what you've done, or what has been done to you. Don't Ever Forget THE Truth. God always sees you, loves you, will never fail you, will never forsake you, can always forgive you, always restore you, and always redeems. God loves you!

Believe the good news. Soul-deep believe, it's true, God loves you—forever, and ever, and ever, and ever, and ever, and ever, and ever…!

I have loved you with an everlasting love. ~ Jeremiah 31:3 ESV

~ *Glory, Hallelujah Footprints* ~

The year was 1958 and Jack, a young seminary student was traveling along a cold, rainy highway when he noticed an elderly man on the side of the road. Without a thought, Jack "tossed" out a prayer on the man's behalf as he drove past.

When Jack arrived at his destination, he discovered his appointment was not available. In a sour mood he began the journey back home. Again he passed the man, who now was on his side of the road, and Jack found himself annoyed with God for not answering his earlier prayer.

Then it dawned on him, perhaps he was the one who needed to give the man a ride. Half-heartedly Jack stopped and backed the distance to where the man stood waiting.

Cringing, Jack sat in the car wondering if the man would be covered in the stench of alcohol or body odor. Instead he found himself pleasantly surprised, at the clean scent, well-shaven, intelligent man who sat next to him.

Thinking perhaps this was an opportunity to witness; Jack turned to his companion to start a conversation. "Lousy weather we're having; isn't it?"

The man smiled kindly, nodded, and looked Jack in the eye. "Son, are you saved?"

The question caught him by surprise and he sat momentarily dumfounded. Words flowed as Jack shared with the man his faith journey, how he had drifted away from God but was brought back through the sweet faith of the young woman who now was his wife.

The man introduced himself as Mr. Doss and told how he walked with the Lord and witnessed to every person he was "supposed to meet that day." He spoke of the Holy Spirit and the Bible. Mentioning he had memorized most of God's word because his eyesight was not great for reading.

"You know," Mr. Doss said with a smile, "I am so happy that when I pick up my left foot it says, Glory and when I pick up the right it says, Hallelujah!"

Jack surveyed the man. "Aren't you lonely?"

Mr. Doss looked at him with surprise. "How could I be lonely?" He continued to tell Jack of his time in prayer, Bible study, and fellowship with the Lord. "How could I be lonely?"

After they parted company, Jack knew he would never be the same man. And to this day he wonders who Mr. Doss really was, especially since on that cold, rainy day, Mr. Doss wasn't even wet.

The story is special to me and my family. Jack is my dad. And someday I'll meet Mr. Doss and we'll walk the glory, hallelujah golden streets and talk about our wonderful God.

My mouth is filled with Your praise and with Your glory all day long. ~ *Psalm 71:8 NASB*

~ Rubbish Gazers ~

The workers are getting tired, and there is so much rubble to be moved. We will never be able to build the wall by ourselves ~ Nehemiah 4:10 NLT.

Are we so busy gazing at the rubbish we've forgotten God's great power? God made the earth by His power. He founded the world by His wisdom and stretched out the heavens by his understanding. ~ Jeremiah 10:12.

Do we think we are too weak or God doesn't have enough power? Not by our might or power, but by My Spirit, says the Lord of hosts. He is able to do immeasurably more than we ask or imagine, according to His power that is at work within us. By His power He will fulfill every good purpose of yours and every act prompted by your faith. We have strength for all things in Christ Who empowers us. We are ready for anything and equal to anything through Him who infuses inner strength into us. We are self-sufficient in Christ's sufficiency. ~ Zechariah 4:6, Ephesians 3:20, 2 Thessalonians 1:11, Philippians 4:13.

Do we think our rubbish heap can't be solved, fixed, rectified, or redeemed by God? Jesus said we will have trouble, but to take heart, He has overcome the world. God made the heaven and earth by His great power and nothing is too difficult for him. Absolutely nothing is impossible for God. ~ John 16:33, Jeremiah 32:17, Matthew 19:26.

Heavenly Father help me to take my eyes off the rubble pile of troubles, the rubbish of my past, and fix my eyes firmly on You and Your power, might, strength, and love. Because nothing is too hard or impossible for You!

~ Thought Control ~

You know those thoughts that ambush from left field, the ones that seem to attack in the middle of the night? Or those thoughts that lead to contemplation on why a situation happened, or something we did wrong, or how someone wronged us–the ones that tailspin our brains into a negative mess? Argh!

The Bible gives us great methods in the battle for the brain by taking every thought captive and renewing our mind. And by making sure we think on whatever is true, whatever is noble, whatever is right, whatever is pure, whatever is lovely, whatever is admirable, excellent or praiseworthy ~ 2 Corinthians 10:5, Romans 12:2, Philippians 4:8.

So when those bad thoughts taunt in the middle of the night or try to creep up during the day, I pounce back with some quick questions — "Does that thought bring me closer to God?" and "Does that thought honor God?" Amazing how quick the enemy flees. We can free up our minds to think on the good things. Take those thoughts under control!

Heavenly Father help me to take my thoughts under control by controlling my thoughts to think about You.

~ *Believing* ~

Believing God is easy on the good days. It's easy to believe God when He does exactly like we expect or want, but believing is much harder in the reality of life.

One of my favorite quotes is by St. Augustine "In my deepest wound, I saw Your glory and it dazzled me." Because through trials, difficulties, detours into sin, I have learned more of God's character, grace, mercy, love, and trustworthiness. They have given me opportunities to better understand who He is and how I fit into His perfect plan.

I still have times I'm hurt, confused, and crawling on wobbly knees. Oh my, some days I feel like I'm swinging on a vine in the jungle, screaming madly. I haven't liked any of those bad moments, but I wouldn't change them for the world, because I see glimpses of His glory in my wounds.

There are layers of belief, going deeper, truly believing God loves us, believing He can be trusted, and believing no matter what happens, takes us to the next level. Not just quick head knowledge, but really, truly believing.

So how do we get there? Don't you wish we could just plug ourselves into some socket in the wall and have everything downloaded to our bodies and brains? Goodness, I'd have the world's largest extension cord.

Fortunately God provides ways for us to understand who He is, and who we are in Him. We have His Spirit in us and we have His word to guide us. Jesus said, if you hold to my teaching you are my disciples and the truth will set you free ~ John 8:31-32.

To hold to Jesus' teaching we have to know what He taught. God's word, how Jesus lived His life, what He said and did, how God reacted with His people, these are methods to learn more of God's heart.

The Bible isn't just words on a page, God's word is alive and active, it's like fire, like a hammer that breaks rocks in pieces. God's word never returns void, is a light for our path, and always accomplishes God's purposes.

There is power in God's word – power to move forward, power to forgive, power to heal, power for today, and power for tomorrow.

Know God and His word, not just snippets but truly know the heart of the author. Knowing enough of whom He is to believe and hold fast to His teachings, knowing His love, experiencing His grace for ourselves and others, and in holding tightly to Him, we find freedom.

Read the Bible, highlight areas about God's character and love. Discover who God is, why certain things happened, how He works. Discover His heart and you'll discover your freedom.

You will guard him and keep him in perfect and constant peace whose mind [both its inclination and its character] is stayed on You, because he commits himself to You, leans on You, and hopes confidently in You. ~ Isaiah 26:3 AMP

~ *Prayer Love* ~

Prayer can and should encompass every moment of our day, regardless of our activities. Prayer isn't a chore, task, or something to be checked off on a to-do list. Prayer isn't rote memorization or only bringing our wants and needs.

Prayer is passion. Prayer is protection; a calm in the storm of life and a safe harbor. Prayer is connecting with The God of the universe, holy, high and exalted, who desires a relationship with each of us, with you.

Prayer is an incredible opportunity to converse with God. Prayer is an amazing blessing to talk with the God of the universe. Prayer is sharing life's joys and difficulties with our Creator.

Prayer is talking and listening. Prayer is spending time with the One who knows you best. No pretenses are needed. God is love. And when you pray you're communicating with love. Prayer is talking with Love, The One who loves you.

My heart has heard you say, 'Come and talk with me.' And my heart responds, 'Lord, I am coming.' ~ Psalm 27:8 NLT

~ Ever-burning Flame ~

There are times I can't feel the light of God's presence. I stumble in the darkness reaching and looking for His hand. My own sinful ways have caused me to turn my back and wander away. Other times I have no clue, all sin is confessed, nothing seems to be hindering my relationship with Him, and I still can't feel His presence. And yet, I wonder if that ever-burning longing isn't part of God's plan.

How else would we know if we have enough faith to walk when we can't sense Him near? How else would we know that we will trust Him even during the difficult trials of life? How else would we know if our faith is only built on emotions? How else would we know that only God can fill our every longing?

I stare at a flickering candle and watch the flame. The candle emits light whether I'm standing in front or looking away. The light remains the same. Our circumstances and emotions change like the wind, but God never changes, He never moves. His grace, mercy, and unfailing love remains. And in our hearts the ever-burning flame burns by the light of His presence.

Heavenly Father thank You that You made the light and You are The Light. Help me remember Your flame never dims.

~ *Trapped Like A Rat* ~

Dressed in footed pajamas, our toddler son held the side of his crib and stared longingly over the rail. He chewed and adjusted the pacifier perched on his lips, hung his head in defeat, and whispered his first complete sentence. "Trapped like a rat."

When our son was young, he had no concern for his safety and would have loved to run and play. Much to his chagrin, at bedtime we kept him in his crib for his protection.

I've heard people say they don't want to become a Christian because they don't want to be "trapped like a rat" in rules and regulations. For them, following God equals loss of freedom to have fun and enjoy life.

The Bible tells us that where the Spirit of the Lord is, there is freedom. But how does that make sense, if God asks us to accept His Son, Jesus Christ as our Savior, and to be in subjection to His authority? Why should we be in subjection to anyone? We want freedom!

Who is God? He is the maker, designer, creator of the universe.

Why should we trust Him? His character traits are Holy, pure and unfailing love, mercy, kindness, faithfulness, gentleness, and a myriad of other perfect and wonderful qualities.

God's parameters on our life are not punishment, but for our protection. Let's take the Ten Commandments as an example.

Number one, have no other gods.
Number two, no idols.
Number three, don't misuse God's name.
Number four, keep the Sabbath Holy (Rest).
Number five, honor your father and mother.
Number six, don't murder.
Number seven, no adultery.
Number eight, don't steal.
Number nine, don't lie or give false testimony.
Number ten, don't covet what someone else has.

Can you imagine how awesome it would be if everyone on this planet honestly and truly lived by the Ten Commandments? The freedom would be amazing. We wouldn't have to worry about being lied to, murdered, or having anything stolen. The Sabbath would truly be a day of rest and relaxation and every facet of our life would be better.

To top off the good news, God knows we aren't perfect, so He put in motion a perfect plan. Jesus Christ, the Son of God, sacrificed His life for us, so that through His grace we can stand before a Holy God.

When God asks us to accept His Son as our Savior, we are no longer trapped like rats. God releases us from the trap of death and sin. God offers hope and a future, freedom from sin and death, freedom to live under God's grace, freedom in His unfailing love, and freedom to experience eternal life.

Heavenly Father we praise You for the glorious grace You have poured out through Your Son, Jesus Christ. Thank You for Your freedom. Thank You that my sins have been forgiven and I can walk free in Your amazing love!

~ Fandangled Fear ~

Scared to death and shaking uncontrollably, our little dog hurried to my chair. He is terrified of thunder and lightning, but the day is sunny and bright. I have no idea what he heard. I hold him close and speak soothing words, and still he shakes. Poor little guy doesn't understand when I tell him he doesn't have to be afraid.

I do the same to God. I hear a noise, or imagine something terrible will happen, and I run to God shaking. If only I'd listen to His words.

I was going to get all theological and list Bible verses, when our little dog placed both paws on the computer and turned to look at me. Methinks he's trying to make a point.

.... Our dog's contribution.

I'll take this thought on a different angle. Do I get in God's way? Does my fear limit what God is trying to do? How often do I allow fear to consume me to the point I can't get anything done (at least nothing worthwhile)?

Fandangled fear blocks the way, way too often.

My pup is still in the way, so I'll end this note with reminders from God's word. God is our God and holds us by our right hand. He says, "Don't fear, I will help you." He is on your side, you don't have to fear, what can mere man do to you? Isaiah 41:13, Psalm 118:6.

Remember God's loving hand is holding you. You don't ever have to allow fandangled fear to block your thoughts, your path, or your life.

~ Who Do You Say I Am? ~

When Jesus came to the region of Caesarea Philippi, he asked his disciples, "Who do people say the Son of Man is?"

The disciples answered, "Some say John the Baptist; others Elijah; and still others, Jeremiah or one of the prophets."

Then Jesus asked, "But what about you? Who do you say I am?" ~ Matthew 16:13-15.

I've been thinking about Jesus' question, *"Who do you say I am?"*

Jesus is first and foremost my Savior. He saved me. He died so that I may live. The older I get, the more life I experience, the deeper the meaning. Every day He shows facets of His amazing, unfailing love.

He is Redeemer, The Way, The Truth, The Life, Compassionate, Forgiving, Champion, Avenger, Defender, Friend, Peace, Joy, Love, Intercessor, Living Water, Strength, Sustainer, Healer, Restorer, Refuge, Righteous Judge, Comforter, Hope, Strong Deliverer, Lover of my soul, oh my the list of His amazing, wonderful qualities are unending.

But how about you?

I'll let Jesus ask the question, *What about you? Who do you say I am?"*

~ *Peace, Be Still* ~

Be still, and know that I am God; I will be exalted among the nations, I will be exalted in the earth! ~ Psalm 46:10 NKJV

Sheets of rain fell while lightning ripped across the sky—I don't know which was worse, the accelerating storm or my rampant fears. Our young son was staying with friends, and my husband had been wheeled down for another test. *Please God bring healing. Protect my family.*

That very moment, a question rose in my spirit: "Will you still love God even if you lost everyone you love?"

It was the end of September 2004. My husband, Dennis, was scheduled for a hip replacement. Due to years of football and running, arthritis had eaten away his cartilage until his hip socket was bone on bone. Surgery went well, and forty-five minutes after his dismissal from the recovery room, therapists had him up and standing.

However Dennis' oxygen levels dropped to drastic levels. Within minutes, nurses and technicians lined the hall outside his room with diagnostic machinery. Each test came back negative and surgeons and doctors were bewildered to find the cause.

Dennis, heavily sedated and blissfully unaware of the danger, was placed on oxygen at increasing levels and his physical therapy halted.

Now I stood at the window of his seventh story hospital room as a major storm moved into the area. I flashbacked years earlier as I had stood at the bedside of my sister-in-law and best friend, Kathy, as she battled leukemia. Wife to my brother, and mom of only a toddler, Kathy battled valiantly for eighteen months. Prayers take on a depth unknown with pain, and although God heard our begging prayers for healing, His divine plan was different from ours. Kathy was taken home to be with the Lord.

Would I still love God—even if I lost everyone?

The choice was mine. I agonized over the possibility of losing everyone, over letting go.

But then, I realized even if everything were removed, God remains unchanging, ever loving, and ever present. Completely undone, I submitted to God's perfect plan. Yes, I would love Him regardless what happened next. Immediately I felt God's presence and pleasure as I clung to Him.

Thankfully Dennis recovered, and our son still remembers the night lightning lit the sky in an amazing display. And I will never forget when God illuminated my soul to believe in His love and peace, no matter what happens next.

Dear Heavenly Father when storms are intense, my fears are big and my faith is so small. Help me to still my soul in Your presence knowing that no matter what happens, You are always good and Your love is always unfailing.

~ Bubble-Wrapped ~

I would prefer all of us lived in little bubbles or were wrapped in bubble wrap. Cars would be bumper cars, planes would bounce instead of crash, and evil and illness wouldn't exist.

And to top it off as we age we would just get cuter and smarter.

Perhaps with eternal reality that is true. We forget our earthly journey is only part of the picture. We age on earth, to be young and our best in Heaven. Oh my, I like that thought.

Jesus repeatedly tells us to not worry about what we have or don't have, or worry about tomorrow because He has overcome the world. He grants us His peace so we don't have to be troubled or afraid. ~ John 16:33, John 14:27.

If we were soldiers with a time machine so we could see the outcome and knew we would win, wouldn't we be amazingly brave?

As Christians, we should be brave. We know the outcome. We will have battles, we might be wounded, we might lose our friends and loved ones, but we know in the end with Christ we win. And we are forever bubble-wrapped soul safe in His presence.

Heavenly Father thank You that even in the battles of life, You are victorious, and we are always, eternally safe in You.

~ Son-Kissed by The Son ~

I meet early every Saturday with a group of women to pray. One morning, the sunrise beckoned us outside as the heavens declared the glory of God. We gathered together singing praises as the sky over the mountains turned from peach to gold. And as we turned to look at one another we could see the glory of the sunrise reflecting on our faces. We were Son-kissed by The Son.

Jesus, the light of the world, came to not only save us but to radiate His glory on us, in us, and through us to a world living in darkness.

Those in Old Testament times saw the manifestation of God's glory – the parting of the Red Sea, the manna, the rescues with God's angelic armies. Over and over again God displayed His glory.

Those who walked with Jesus saw the manifestations of His glory, through His life, miracles, and His resurrection.

As Christians we are given not only the knowledge of His manifestation, we are given the glorious manifestation of His presence living within us. What joy!

Don't you love looking at the moon? Isn't it amazing to know that the moon has no light, it only reflects the sun. We too can reflect The Heavenly Son's glory. Not just reflect but radiate God's love.

A prism only looks like a cut piece of glass, but when the light hits, the prism radiates a bounty of colors. We are God's prisms reflecting the glorious colors of His light throughout our world.

I love taking photos. The better the lighting, the better the shot. Have you ever tried to take a photo in a dark environment? Not much shows up. However if you use the flash, things light up and can be seen.

God's light flashes with the grace from Jesus Christ to radiate in our lives. Looking at His light, focusing on Him, and His blessings gives us new eyes lighting up our world.

When you step outside, if you look at the sun, your face radiates with the warmth of the sunshine. However if you turn away, the shadows stretch in front of you. We miss so much if we choose to look at the shadows of life instead of the Heavenly Son.

Heavenly Father help me to stay in Your Son-Shine where I am Son-kissed by Your Son!

~ *Pride Check* ~

Yesterday I assisted a friend at a business convention. Not sure how much I helped other than manning her booth during the lunch hour, but I did enjoy visiting with her and others. I felt rather confident in my spiffy new shirt and slacks as I greeted business people.

Until this morning, when I had the oddest feeling perhaps I had spent the day with the zipper of my pants down.

Maybe too much information for a few of you, but my fear is rooted in the fact a booth across from us had several ladies looking our way and laughing. I know my friend looked great, so it wasn't her. Perhaps they were laughing at jokes and their gaze just naturally fell in our direction.

Or maybe ... it *was* me. Argh! Attack of the major insecurities.

I shouldn't have been so confident. And worse, maybe my confidence was rooted in pride. Ugh. The dreaded "P" word. The Bible reminds us, A man's pride brings him low, and when pride comes, then comes disgrace ~ Proverbs 29:23, 11:2. The thought of being confident/prideful with my zipper down sure has left me feeling rather low and disgraceful. Ouch. Whimper.

I'm not crazy at all about these humiliating emotions. However I am grateful for the reminder to always check zipper before leaving home. And always, always, always, always, always, always, make sure confidence doesn't take a painful side trip toward pride.

Dear Heavenly Father, thank you for the pride check. Please help me stay grounded in You. And always remember that any confidence comes from You alone, for I am nothing without Your grace, mercy, and love.

~ Sheltered In His Arms ~

The call came late at night. 'One of the boys is missing ... It's Jack.' Hastily, my dad put on his coat and drove to the Boy's Home where he worked as Executive Director. Rain and ice pelted the car and the windshield wipers brushed away furrows of frost. The tires struggled for traction on a glazing coat of ice covering the bridge.

The Christian home offered refuge and safety for children and Jack was one of their best kids. Dad arrived at the home. Shielding his head, he dashed for the covered porch. Nothing had changed, the boy was still missing. Grabbing a slicker to put over his coat, he stepped back into the rain.

That week, Jack had been given a new calf by the ranch manager and told if he cared for the calf properly, the animal would be his.

Flashlight in hand, my father ran and slipped his way to the fenced area at the barn where the calves were kept. Icy rain slid down his neck as he searched for Jack's calf. Dad climbed the fence to look farther and stumbled over a broken bale of hay. After spotting a crumpled coat on the ground, he reached to pick it up. His throat tightened as salty tears mixed with rain.

Inside the coat, Jack lay asleep. His back to the rain, ice crystals forming on his jacket, he sheltered the only thing he had ever owned of value—a small red calf.

Years later, my dad continues to share this true story. Other than groggy and cold, Jack was fine. And the calf received the royal treatment with a bed made from bales of hay. Like Jack did his young calf, God wraps us tightly in His love, protecting us through the storms and cold of this world.

You are cherished by the God of the universe. No difficulty or problem will ever keep Him from your side.

Heavenly Father thank You that we are safely sheltered forever in Your loving arms.

~ *Paramedic Angels* ~

Undiagnosed torn ligaments and tendons caused a nightmare of unbearable pain. Doctors would only scratch their heads and send me home with increasing dosages of pain medicine. One evening during prayer time our young son prayed for "Paramedic Angels." The next night he prayed for angelic ambulances.

The following day I visited an orthopedic surgeon. He poked and prodded, gave a quick cortisone shot in the ailing hip, and sent me home with a prescription for physical therapy. Still hurting but grateful for a non-surgical diagnosis, I hobbled to my car and called friends and family on my cell phone.

After my conversations, I remembered something I had left inside the doctor's office. Limping inside I picked up the item and returned to the car. My keys were not in my purse. Unfortunately, I found them—firmly locked in the car and still in the ignition.

The call was made for an auto service, and I went back inside. While staring out the lobby window I watched, waited, and prayed. A fire truck and ambulance pulled up with lights flashing. The paramedics jumped out, wheeled in a gurney, and a few minutes later returned with a man to transport to the hospital.

After they had the man safely in the ambulance and on his way, I explained my predicament to one of the remaining firemen. A few minutes later my car was unlocked, and after a round of thanks I was on my way.

Then I remembered my son's prayer. Paramedic angels had come to my aid. I drove home, praising God for loving us through the pain, and through silly mistakes. Thankfully, no prayer request is overlooked, and no prayer is thought trite or silly. All we have to do is ask.

Heavenly Father thank You that Your word promises that You command Your angels to guard us in all your ways. ~ Psalm 91:11

~ Bunny Bustin'~

Just as a father has compassion on his children, so the LORD has compassion on those who fear Him. For He Himself knows our frame; He is mindful that we are but dust. ~ Psalm 103:13-14 NASB

My husband adjusted the super-sized ladder to the highest setting, then handed our super-tall son the extendable duster. His assignment? Clean the tallest ledge inside our home.

Dust bunnies cowered as our son climbed to the top of the ladder, stretched his long, lean arms, and annihilated any and all hidden dust creatures. Every ledge, shelf, cabinet top, nook and cranny, succumbed to the Bunny Bustin' Buffaloes.

Cleaning is never-ending. How can one small Buffaloe herd make so many messes, and where does all that dust come from? I'm still waiting for the invention of the wash-and-wear house.

I must admit, I have personal dust problems. I've wallowed in my share of slimy sin pits, and I can't even claim ignorance. I knew better. Unfortunately sin doesn't always appear "that" dirty and often looks appealing. However one step in the sin, and sin rolls along like small dust particles, collecting other sins, until the grimy soul dust bunnies invade every crevice. More than a duster is needed to remove that kind of dirt and grime.

Fortunately our sins can be washed through the forgiveness, grace, and mercy of Jesus Christ. And when Jesus sweeps into our lives, He dusts us off, and busts away sin's filth.

Thank You Heavenly Father for Your amazing love and compassion that reaches out to messy humanity and offers a way for redemption. Thank You, Jesus that sin's dust bunnies are forever blown away by Your thorough soul cleansing.

~ *Would You Be Willing?* ~

One of my friends asked what people thought about the rapture (Jesus returning for His believers).

Would the rapture happen before the tribulation, during, or after? The replies were rather interesting. Several people took very firm stances. Each had their opinions on what they believed would happen to those who have a relationship with Christ during the end times.

I'm not going to give you my thoughts. But I will pose some questions.

Would you be willing to trust in God's goodness, even if times get difficult? Will you stand firm in your beliefs even if you are persecuted? Would you be willing to go through a time of tribulation if it meant more people were brought to God's kingdom? Would you be willing to be martyred to save the lost?

How far will we go, how much pain will we endure, how much suffering is worth saving a soul?

Would you, will you, be willing to give yourself to save someone else?

Dear one, no greater love is given than one who lays down his life for his friends. ~ John 15:1

~ *Where Is The Control?* ~

When I worked in the computer field, I absolutely loved my job. I designed systems and programmed computers to do my bidding. If something didn't work, each line of code could be analyzed and then corrected. There was always a way to accomplish each goal. The thrill of victory and ultimate control!

Then, our son was born. He didn't come with source code. He wasn't programmable. He didn't sleep. He was very active. He didn't sleep. He didn't have a mute button, he didn't sleep, he was very active, he didn't sleep, he was very, very active, and did I mention he didn't sleep?

Where was the source code, the programmers guide, and the instruction book? What happened to my control?

Everyone generously shared their advice on babies, but no one knew our individual needs or the needs of our child. Fortunately, God had (and has) the answer -- all the answers. He has the codes, instructions, and He is our guide. He made each of us, and knows what works and what does not. God is the maker and designer.

When I released control, God could work without me getting in the way. And in the freedom of allowing God to lead, I learned how to enjoy our smart, witty, amazing, incredible, fun son.

Heavenly Father thank You that You are in control. Help me to relinquish control to You in every part of my life and the lives of others around me. Thank You that You have everything under control!

~ Reboot ~

Ever been working on a project and your computer freezes? Total shut down. Overloaded and locked up tight. No matter what you do, nothing works. There is no other option but to turn off the computer and reboot. And if you're lucky, the system resumes and you start fresh.

The other night I woke and a zillion thoughts and worries threatened to overload my little brain. I tried to corral them, but to no avail. With a shut down imminent, I cried out to God for a thought reboot with His word.

Verses from Psalm 23 and Psalm 121 came to mind. I lift up my eyes to the hills. From where does my help come? My help comes from the LORD, who made heaven and earth. The LORD is my shepherd; I shall not want. He makes me lie down in green pastures. He leads me beside still waters. He restores my soul. ~ Psalm 121:1-2, Psalm 23:1-3 ESV

Thoughts, worries, and fears rampaging? System break-down imminent? Reboot with God's healing word restoration.

Heavenly Father when life is overwhelming and my thoughts run rampant, help me to reboot with Your healing, restoring word.

~ Unsheathing The Sword ~

I thought I effectively utilized the sword of the Spirit through studying scriptures, Bible study, and church attendance. During spiritual battle, I would pray in my mind to God for His protection, guidance, and wisdom. Yet I often felt rather bloodied after spiritual attacks. One night I felt God's Spirit prompt me to verbalize my prayer. At first I hesitated not sure why, yet as the words were released into the air the power came forth.

God spoke the world into existence. His words carry the ultimate power. And when we speak His words, we are unleashing His power and authority.

I'm sure the enemy appreciated when I kept quiet, because my sheathed sword remained infective. The enemy can't read our mind. He listens and watches intently to our words and actions. Satan can bombard us with thoughts to try to twist the truth, but he can't be rebuked unless we speak the words. Verbalizing God's word gives us protection, and once that sword is unsheathed God's power flows mightily forth.

Heavenly Father help me to unsheathe my sword of the Spirit. Help me always remember that strength and ability come from the Your word. Help me to use and verbalize Your scripture, for Your words carry power. Help me to know them, love them, use them, and live them.

Those who love Your law have great peace, And nothing causes them to stumble. ~ Psalm 119:165 NAS

~ *Only You* ~

God loves you – just as you are ... wounded, battered, and bruised. God loves you – your past, the hidden things no one knows. God loves you – the scars that carved and left jagged valleys in your soul. God loves you and no one and nothing can keep Him from you.

No person. No power on earth. No memory. No flashback. No sin. No thought. No action. Nothing can stop God from offering His healing, and His everlasting, unfailing love.

Only you.

Only you can accept, His forgiveness. His healing. His mercy. His grace. His pure love. His joy. His peace of mind.

God loves you. God chose freely to love you. Only you can accept what He freely offers. Only you can turn the ears of your soul to hear His call. God is calling. No matter what you have done. No matter what has been done against you. Regardless how deep the stain of sin, or how messed up the life, God's arms are open wide.

And God wants you. No one else will do. No one else has been created like you. No one else can fulfill the divine purpose for which you have been created. Only you.

Heavenly Father it's me. Only me. Thank You that You love me, every part of only me.

~ *Word Menu* ~

An actor's taped conversations with his ex-girlfriend were repeatedly played by the press, talk-show hosts, and YouTube. Regardless of how you felt about the actor, his unsavory words resulted in a huge mess.

I have yet to meet a person not deeply affected by someone's words. Every word spoken has consequences. Words can cut like a knife or soothe the soul. Words reveal our character and how we feel about life and others.

Words also go beyond human ears. Satan and his nasty minions are always listening, recording our speech and our reactions. And boy, howdy are they ready to pounce on anything negative.

Gossip, lies, slander, rudeness, and any negative talk, weighs us down, keeps us out of communion with God, and attracts Satan like buzzards on road kill.

God's word, thankfulness, and praise, puts a spring in our step, brings us closer to God, and sends the enemy scurrying for cover.

So what's on your word menu for today?

Words satisfy the mind as much as fruit does the stomach; good talk is as gratifying as a good harvest. Words kill, words give life; they're either poison or fruit—you choose. ~ Proverbs 18:20-21 MSG.

Let the words of my mouth and the meditation of my heart be acceptable in your sight, O Lord, my rock and my redeemer. For by your words you will be justified, and by your words you will be condemned. ~ Psalm 19:14, Matthew 12:37 ESV

~ Heart-Check ~

Have you given your heart to Christ? Not just head knowledge, but heart knowledge. We can't enter heaven on our upbringing, church affiliation, or our "goodness."

Years ago, I worked in a company as an IT specialist. A man in one of the departments spouted all the latest buzzwords for computer technology and programming. Upper management was impressed and thought he was wonderful.

The man's knowledge was mere lip service. He talked a good game, but knew nothing of the realities of working with the system. He made my job a nightmare. Every day I would have to search and find areas where he had messed with source code. No one believed me ... until I left the company. Within a few weeks, the man was fired for making an absolute shambles of the company's software programs.

Claiming to be a Christian is mere lip service without a personal relationship with Christ. According to the Barna Group*, the percentage of adults who describe themselves as Christian is 84%. Yet, the percentage of adults who can be classified as born again Christians, based on their belief that they will experience eternal salvation based on their commitment to Jesus Christ, personal confession of sin, and acceptance of Christ as their savior, is only 40%.

Are you a Christian? Please know what you claim. Please make sure. Don't wait another moment. The benefits are eternal and so are the risks. Matthew 15:8-9 Jesus warns of those who honor Him with their lips but their hearts are far from Him. John 14:6 Jesus tells us that He is the way, the truth, and the life, and no one comes to the Father except through Jesus.

There is no Christianity without Christ. Even knowing Jesus Christ is God's Son, doesn't lead to salvation. Even the demons know and believe that fact (and tremble).

Words are not enough, and idle claims are not enough. Relationship with Christ and through making Jesus the Lord of our lives is the only way to heaven. Not just head knowledge belief, but heart knowledge leading to soul deep believing.

Please do a heart check. Make sure.

Do you know, really know Christ as Savior and Lord of your life?

I know the one in whom I trust, and I am sure that he is able to guard what I have entrusted to him until the day of his return. ~ *2 Timothy 1:12 NLT*

*http://www.barna.org/faith-spirituality/504-barna-examines-trends-in-14-religious-factors-over-20-years-1991-to-2011

~ *The Worst That Could Happen?* ~

Do you worry? Fret? Agonize? Do you allow the worry to run rampant, disturbing your day and unsettling your sleep? What is the worst that could happen? Take that worry, take it to the end.

Lots of terrible things can happen. I understand. I know. But what happens in the end? The very end.

Death of a dream. Death of a loved one. Death of a situation ... Death

Death is never the end. New doors open. New life is given. New hope comes. Even in physical death, the soul remains. Death is not the end.

And in death, if you're a Christian, you are winged to heaven's door. To your perfect home where there is no more sickness, no more pain, no more worry, no fear, no tears of agony, nothing bad, and no evil. Joy, peace, love, love, and more love. And those loved ones you will leave behind? God will be there for them. God will provide. God will comfort. God will bring peace.

If you're not a Christian, you still have time. You can still say yes to God's Son, Jesus Christ. There is a place for you too. Heaven's doors are open wide and waiting.

If you're afraid to make that leap, afraid to become a Christian ... what is the worst that could happen?

Take it to the end. The very end.

God so loved the world that He gave His only Son, that whoever believes in Him won't perish but have everlasting life. For God did not send His Son into the world to condemn the world, but that the world, through Him might be saved. If you declare with your mouth, "Jesus is Lord," and if you believe in your heart that God raised Jesus from the dead, you will be saved. Anyone who believes and is baptized will be saved. But anyone who refuses to believe will be condemned. If anyone's name was not found written in the book of life, he was thrown into the lake of fire. ~ John 3:16-17, Romans 10:8-9, Mark 16:16, Revelation 20:15

~ The Gift Of Grace ~

As a teenager I wondered what the top speed was for my little car. A two-lane farm road afforded the opportunity. I decided to put the pedal to the metal. Yep, I stuck my foot on the gas and flew down the road. That little engine whined and screamed.

And that's when I saw him, the patrol car sitting on the side of the road. I was caught. It had to be obvious. How many little Toyotas whiz by at break-neck speed? The first opportunity to stop was a gravel road leading to a farmhouse. I pulled over and waited.

The patrol car stopped behind me; no lights and no siren. The officer just sat in his car.

A few minutes later he approached my open window. "Do you live here?"

I kept my hands on the wheel. "No sir."

"You just pulled over?"

"Yes sir."

His face showed no emotion, his eyes hidden behind mirrored sunglasses. "What were you doing?"

"I was trying to see how fast my car would go."

He didn't move for a few minutes. Finally, he shook his head. "Don't do it again." And with that, he turned and walked away.

I deserved to get a ticket. I even admitted my crime. Although I was guilty, I was pardoned and given the gift of grace.

Two thousand years ago, a baby boy was born in Bethlehem, and at His birth the heavens rejoiced and Earth found hope. For this wasn't any ordinary boy; His name is Jesus, and He is the Son of God. He came to Earth to sacrifice His life to redeem the lost and pardon the guilty.

Jesus offers the ultimate gifts each and every day—grace and mercy; all we must do is believe.

For all have sinned and fall short of the glory of God, and are justified by his grace as a gift, through the redemption that is in Christ Jesus.~ Romans 3:23-24 ESV

~ Feasting ~

Blessed are those who hunger and thirst for righteousness, for they shall be filled. ~ Matthew 5:6 NKJV

I'm so hungry and thirsty, Lord. So desperate for Your presence. Family and friends are precious, yet can never soul-satisfy.

I wake in the night and cry out Your name. Where are You Lord?

In the day, I search for You. And my soul is so lonely. So very lonely, desperately hungry for You. And in that loneliness, I turn my eyes to You.

Your Word beckons, *Come, read, and see how Your God loves you so.*

And my spirit voices thanks to The One who never will leave or forsake, the One who loves with unfailing love.

A praise song draws my soul to the knees. And my arms lift in praise. And praise drives away the enemy and His lies.

For in Your Word, in praise, and in thanksgiving we find You.

You were never gone. You never leave us. Your Word speaks of Your love, and my soul feasts on You.

For You O Lord fill to the brim those who hunger and thirst for You.

We praise You Father. Our hands lift in praise as You drive away and defeat the enemy. Thank You Father for Your lavish, unfailing love. Thank You that we are never alone. Let us feast on Your Word, draw near with thanksgiving, and rest in the safety of Your mighty hands.

~ Bobble-Head Buffaloe ~

I have a normal brain—well, at least according to the latest MRI. Unfortunately, my neck is a mess. Five out of seven discs are described with discouraging words such as degeneration, protrusion, bulging, desiccation, compression, kyphosis, indents the cord, severe bilateral foraminal narrowing ... I'm grateful two out of the five discs are still normal.

At time my body holds the rest of me hostage. To be candid, it's frustrating. I don't know if it's pride or sheer stubbornness, but I want to show God and everyone else I'm strong—so I push through. I pushed and kept pushing until I could no longer push.

It is here God met me. In spite of struggles, God's presence comes, calling to rely totally on Him. He is all I need. He is the source of strength and through Him all things are possible.

I'm not alone in this journey. Most of you are hurting. We flounder in our own worlds, our own pain, and our own problems. At times we've simply spread ourselves too thin. And I wonder if we miss the blessing of extending our arms to fully receive what God offers.

Jesus says for those who are weary and burdened to come to Him and He gives rest. Soul rest. The daily struggle doesn't have to be such a struggle. We don't have to carry burdens alone. We weren't designed to plow through life without help. The world doesn't rest on our shoulders or rely on our strength. Jesus tells us to cast our cares on Him because God's strength is available and limitless.

God is in control. I don't have to worry if my neck falls off, and I'm left as a bobble-head Buffaloe. God will carry me through and provide what I need. We can rely and rest on His strength. He will also carry you. His shoulders are broad enough to carry us all.

Heavenly Father, thank You for Your strength. Regardless of health, life, bobble-heads, busyness, family, or circumstances, You are all-powerful, free-flowing, universe creating, death-defying, unlimited strength.

~ *Growth Pains* ~

Our son stands tall at six foot eight inches, and may still be growing. His knees ache with growth pains. Oh my. I've passed the fifty mark and my body is also changing. Whimper. I am not fond of the outward changes, but the internal growth makes the journey into aging worthwhile.

I do want to be further along in spiritual growth. The more I pray to be closer, to see His face, to dwell in His presence, the more amazing the journey, and the more heartbreaking.

Because, I have sooooo much to learn. So much needed growth, so many rough edges to be shaved off and removed. Growth pain leaves me weeping and grateful for God's faithful and continuous grace, mercy, and love.

I don't want to keep getting older without my soul growing. I don't want to be stagnant or left floundering in my own limited knowledge, because there is so ... much ... to ... learn.

Heavenly Father, thank You that You continue working with us until Christ Jesus returns. We are dirt and clay, You are the potter. We are metal, You are the silversmith. You promise to complete what You has started and finish Your work. Mold us and make us into the image of Your wonderful Son. Longing for growth, we stretch out our hands to You.

~ Heart-Nudge ~

There are days when I'm not sure what I'm supposed to do. Those days are a struggle. I want an agenda. For God to say, "Lisa, today I want you to do this."

The other morning my day started, and I felt the nudge to clean the kitchen floor. The thought struck me as odd since my floor wasn't dirty. But the pressing continued. So I grabbed a wet rag and went to my knees.

With praise music playing in the background, I started cleaning. And during the project, I realized ... oh my goodness ... I was having the best time! There on my knees, I was praising, praying, praising some more, and oh I could feel God's pleasure. His heart nudge was never about the floor. God wanted me to spend time with Him. How amazing!

And I think about the people I love, my family and friends, the people I want to spend time with, and the special moments when we commune one-on-one. Precious time to talk, laugh, pray, and encourage one another.

God loves you. He thinks about you non-stop. He longs to connect, and His love beckons.

When you have the urge to pick up your Bible, or sense a gentle tap on the shoulder of your soul, that is God calling to your heart. God calls, beckoning to know Him and be known. How will you respond to the quiet longing and stirring in your soul, the sweet beckoning to your heart to intertwine with God's heart? The gentle request to pull away from the busyness of life and come before His throne.

Have you felt the tender fluttering within? A quiet longing and stirring in your soul. A sweet beckoning to your heart to intertwine with His heart. A gentle request to pull away from the busyness of life and come before God's throne. God wants to spend time with you. Yes, even you.

If you hear God's call, if you feel that nudge, go spend time with Him. Nothing on earth matches the awesome, amazing blessing of being in God's presence.

Heavenly Father how my soul longs for Your presence. Thank You for the yearning that comes from You. My soul has heard You call, and I am Yours.

~ Molting ~

I'm a work in progress. I told my Bible study friends I feel like I'm covered in scales highlighted for removal. There is an awakening of flaws that need to be pried off and eliminated.

Maybe as a Buffaloe I'm molting.

The more I seek God and pursue His presence through prayer and Bible study, the more my imperfections are revealed through gentle nudges or light bulb, "aha" moments. I've stopped in my tracks shocked to find something that has lurked for years in some dark recess. We are talking a major God-directed spring cleaning.

And the oddly, wonderfully giddy thing is, with each spot peeled away, cleaned up, and released to God's healing/restoring touch, the more I find freedom.

While writing this devotion I remembered something that happened when I was a teenager. My dad had requested I clean the kitchen. I scrubbed counters, mopped the floor, and cleaned the stove and sink. Once I was sure I had done a fairly good job, I announced the job was complete. My dad gave the kitchen a cursory glance and asked if I was sure I had done a really good job. I nodded. He asked again. Now I worried, but said "yes." Without further comment, he walked to the counter, picked up a canister and pointed to the money he had earlier placed underneath. Ouch and bummer.

Because of my lack of diligence, I had missed the prize.

Heavenly Father, thank You for shining the light of Your truth on areas in my life that need cleaning. Please keep working on me, help me to be diligent to scrub away anything that keeps me from growing closer to You – the ultimate prize.

~ *What We Would Have Missed* ~

The Buffaloe herd remained in an apartment for ten months while we waited for our Texas house to sell. We knew without a doubt the move was God ordained, but we were surprised our house stayed on the market. We had waited so long between jobs, why did we continue to wait for the house to sell? I wanted all my belongings and to be settled in a home. I was so ready to nest.

Even with the questions, we knew we were abundantly blessed. Our Saturdays were spent driving to explore Idaho. Every weekend was a new adventure. We've climbed the highest sand dunes in North America, seen breathtaking canyons, waterfalls, prairie dog villages that stretch for miles, rivers, valleys, and mountains.

We found a new church home and made new friends. And to top off the blessings, our time together as a family has been priceless.

If my son and I had stayed behind in Texas waiting for the house to sell, I would have worked myself to death trying to think of ways to make the house more sellable. I would have stewed that I was away from my sweet husband, and my health would have undoubtedly suffered.

We would have missed the Idaho trees budding into spring, watching the snow melt off the mountains, and experiencing the beauty of summer. We would have missed our family time together, talking, and laughing. We would have missed seeing God's amazing, wonderful scenery.

Most of all, we would have missed resting in God's sufficiency. How grateful I am for the waiting, when the waiting is to watch what God will do.

Those who wait for the LORD will gain new strength; they will mount up with wings like eagles, they will run and not get tired, they will walk and not become weary. ~ *Isaiah 40:31 NASB*

~ *What Am I Supposed To Do?* ~

I've been really trying to fight off a heavy feeling of being out of sync and out of sorts. I keep thinking I need to write more, be more, perform more, speak more, do more, and instead just keep spinning the wheels of my muddied-up brain.

So I started wondering, what really is important? What do I truly need to accomplish? Jesus tells us to Love the Lord your God with all your heart and with all your soul and with all your mind and with all your strength. And His last words to His disciples were, to Go into all the world and preach the good news.

Hmmm. Okay, I can work on those things. But what about those days where the body and brain have the energy of a comatose slug?

That's when Nehemiah 8:10 jumped in my tiny, barely active brain, the joy of the Lord will make you strong.

Yowza, how cool is that? Instead of worrying and mulling about "me," this little ole me should be focusing on God. Not just focusing, but whole-heartedly loving God and enjoying Him— which has the rebound affect of strengthening body and soul. And then get to work telling others and spreading the good news.

I'll share a fun To Do List...

Seek first the kingdom of God
Believe
Have faith
Forgive
Don't judge
Take every thought captive
Walk worthy
Run with perseverance
Count it all joy when facing trials
Don't worry
Rejoice always
Praise God
Be thankful

Count and recount blessings
God is merciful, be merciful
God is love, be loving
God is compassionate, be compassionate
God is giving, be generous
God is holy, be holy
God is light, share The light
Jesus is the bread of life, share His nourishment
Jesus is truth, share The truth
Jesus is The Way, show others The Way
Share the Good News
Jesus is coming back, always be ready!

~ Sapped ~

The bed clings, pulling me deeper into the comfort of warm sheets. The floor is littered with tissues. Empty cough drop wrappers adorn the nightstand. I don't want to get up.

Some cold/sinus nasty/please-don't-let-it-be-flu thing has infiltrated my body. If I take something to end the dripping nose, my head throbs and swells like a balloon. My eyes leak and my nose resembles a certain reindeer. I hate things that sap my strength and keep me from accomplishing what needs to be done.

My present problems are nothing in the grand scheme of things. This too will pass. There have been other times I wasn't so sure, times I couldn't get out of bed without someone to help or carry.

Life is full of those stop-in-the-tracks moments, or side-slips into a messy mire of difficulties and trials. Some things pass quickly, others are life-changing and altering. They don't go away, and if we aren't careful, despair wraps like a wet cement cloak across the shoulders. It's hard not to worry about tomorrow and what will come.

Jesus teaches us to pray, "Give us this day our daily bread." Bread enough for today. He will feed and supply all our needs. He tells us not to worry about tomorrow, because He will be with us as we go through life. He will never leave or forsake us. His mercies are new every morning. And even when our strength is sapped, God will give us the grace we need, the strength we need, and all the love we need.

Heavenly Father, help me to remember that faith isn't about my body's strength, but by casting my worn-out, ailing body on Your universe-carrying, amazing, loving, unfailing broad shoulders.

~ *You Were Worth It All* ~

Jesus felt pain and suffering. He knows how hard and evil this life could be. For thirty-three years, he walked in our shoes. Then He made the ultimate sacrifice—His own life.

Jesus knew the terrors of the cross. He had seen others crucified, heard their cries, saw the slow, humiliating, and agonizing death. The God-man in His humanity knew what awaited Him. The night before His crucifixion, He cried out to His Abba Father, begging for another way. Yet He willingly submitted to what must be done.

Soldiers trained in warfare and combat beat Jesus, and every hit carried the fury of hell. Beaten until unrecognizable, He underwent the agony of the cross. And then the perfect, sinless, Son of God underwent unbearable pain as every sin ever committed rested on His shoulders.

Why did Jesus go to the cross? Why did He allow the suffering and pain? Why didn't He call the angels to destroy us all?

You.

God doesn't ever want to live without you. The suffering, pain, and heartache throughout His life was worth it because He knew you would need a Savior. What made the cross worth the pain?

You.

Jesus, I'm so amazed and humbled that You went through the agony and suffering of the cross for me. Thank You, Jesus. Thank You for the sacrifice You made for my freedom.

~ Laying Down The Flesh ~

It's easy to wear hang-dog expressions and live a defeated life because life is downright difficult. We drag our woes behind on invisible chains, or pack then in our proverbial backpacks, wearing the fragrance of every stink bomb ever thrown by the enemy.

I've been trapped in the "me, myself, and I" mode. I have days, weeks, months, ahem ... years, I struggled with past issues. Not just what I've been through, but what I've done. The past would rear its ugly head in the daylight; others crept into dreams in the night, leaving me struggling to regain a firm footing.

When we step into the Christian life we are to die to self. Lay down the flesh. Life ceases to be about me, myself, and I, I, I, I....

Because when we focus only on our needs, all we see are our needs, and we miss others needs. When we focus only on ourselves, we miss seeing blessings, and we miss being a blessing. When we focus only on our abilities, we miss the ability to see beyond our abilities to see God's abilities.

When we focus only on our flesh, coddling the flesh, wanting the flesh to save, we miss The Savior. When we focus on our self, we are locked in self-pity, self-entitlement, and self-reliance, and we miss the blessings of dying to self to fully live in Christ. When we focus on God and exalt God, the more we see His provision, His blessings, His abilities, His saving grace, might, and abundant life.

Heavenly Father, help me to lay down me so I can be filled with You!

~ The Stink Bomber ~

We live in a fallen world and we have an enemy. And our enemy is no gentleman; he hits below the belt and kicks when we are down. Satan will use every trick in the book to either keep you from the saving grace found in Christ or try to make you as ineffective as possible.

Satan knows our hidden wounds (since he was the instigator). The enemy uses past hurts to question God's goodness and our worth as a person and to isolate us from others and from God. The last thing the enemy wants is our total freedom, and he works hard to convince us we should keep some things hidden and locked away.

God's word reminds us our enemy prowls like a roaring lion looking for someone to devour. (1 Peter 5:8). But remember, Satan is a defeated foe. Through Jesus, the enemy has been declawed and defanged. Don't let a conquered enemy gum you to death.

Through Christ and His power we are free. Christ came to set the captives free. God is not a part-time-God or part-time-redeemer and restorer. Jesus' grace, mercy, and healing are free, full, and complete. Jesus has overcome the world, and when He lives inside of us, we live as overcomers. Need stink bomb remover? Get Jesus!

My dear children, you belong to God and have defeated them; because God's Spirit, who is in you, is greater than the devil, who is in the world. ~ 1 John 4:4 NCV

~ Whispered Comfort ~

Lightning flashes and thunder reverberates in the room. Wide-eyed and tail down, our little dog runs to my chair. Whispering words of comfort, I scoop him into my arms and cradle his shaking body. He looks at me with puppy dog eyes as if to question why I don't fix things, and why I don't stop the frightening noises.

I hate that he's afraid. The weather radar shows the storm is only a rain shower. I whisper encouragement and hold him close. If only he could understand my words, he would know he was safe.

Holding him, I wonder how often I've run to God, wanting Him to dispel scary things and make life all better. I've often cried to Him when evil touched my life, or worries regarding health, job, children, family, and friends became overwhelming. I try to show my dog how much I love him and that he can trust me to keep him safe. God knows we also get afraid and need His tender touch.

No matter how difficult the day, God's voice speaks through His Word with encouragement and hope. Don't fear, I'm with you. Don't be dismayed, I am your God. I will provide strength and help you. I will hold you with my hand. I am the Lord, your God, who takes your hand and say, don't fear. I will help you. ~ Isaiah 41:10,13.

Storms will blow, but God's comfort is found in the whisper of His loving words.

For the mountains may be removed and the hills may shake, but My lovingkindness will not be removed from you, and My covenant of peace will not be shaken, says the LORD who has compassion on you. ~ Isaiah 54:10 NASB.

~ On Mission ~

If you are a Christian, did you realize you are on mission? If you're still breathing, you are blessed with a purpose. Not a day or moment is wasted by God. You don't have to go overseas, write a best-selling book, have the biggest blog followers, or be on the evening news to leave an eternal legacy.

Did you realize one prayer for that lost person may be the one prayer that helps tip their heart open to God?

Did you know that one smile you gave the person at the grocery store may have saved their life?

Did you know your difficult work situation, home life, or illness you face is being watched by a hurting world? Someone is watching.

Someone is longing to find a life that will speak life in the midst of pain. Someone needs to know your Savior.

Tell others. Tell them about Jesus Christ, The Savior. The Savior who touches hurting lives. The Savior who walks on water in the storms. The Savior who restores what the enemy tries to destroy. The Savior who loves beyond earthly comprehension. The Savior who holds arms open wide for all who will come.

Be on mission, be available. The rewards are eternal.

The most important thing is that I complete my mission, the work that the Lord Jesus gave me—to tell people the Good News about God's grace.~ Acts 20:24 NCV

~ There Is Nothing ~

Whom have I in heaven but you? And there is nothing on earth that I desire besides you. ~ Psalm 73:25ESV

There is nothing I have given God He has not returned in abundance.
There is nothing I have done, or has been done to me, that God's grace and mercy has not restored and redeemed.
There is nothing I can offer God but me.
And He takes my nothingness, tenderly cradles my heart, soothes and heals the scars, and binds the broken places with His love.
There is nothing in this life without Him.
There is nothing I want more than more of Him.

Thank You Father, for taking my nothing and giving me Your everything.

~ CIA - Christians in Action ~

Living true Christianity requires action. Jesus says if you love Me, you'll obey Me. And to be honest, it's not always easy being a Christian. Fortunately, the Bible has action words to help us along our journey.

Lift up your eyes and your heads.
Take courage.
Be strong.
Stand firm.
Let the peace of Christ rule in your hearts.
Carry your cross.
Follow your Savior.
Cast your cares on the Lord.
Let the words of Christ dwell in you richly.
Put on the full armor of God – *Take up* the shield of faith, sword of the Spirit, and helmet of salvation.
Be thankful and *Think* on the good things.
Rejoice as you take refuge in Christ, knowing your journey leads straight to Heaven's door.

So don't just be a Christian, be a Christian In Action, join the CIA!

Heavenly Father, I don't want to only be a Christian, I want to be part of the CIA!

~ John 14:15, Psalm 121:1, Luke 21:28, Matthew 14:27, 1 Corinthians 16:13, Colossians 3:15, Luke 14:27, Psalm 55:22, Colossians 3:16, Ephesians 6:11, 16-17, Philippians 4:6, 4:4, Psalm 46:10, 1 Peter 4:13.

~ *Put Down The Flesh And Back Away Quickly!* ~

I have a confession. I have flesh. Yes, I am a fleshly creature. And the older I get, the more my flesh is losing its once tight texture. My flesh is falling. Bummer.

But ya know, that might not be such a bad thing. My flesh is temporary, and my flesh gets in the way of living an abandoned life for God.

Paul makes some great points in Romans 8. When we live in the flesh, our minds are on fleshly things. When we live in the Spirit, our mind is set on the Spiritual things.

Flesh = death. Spirit = eternal life.

Looks like an easy decision. I choose to live in God's Spirit, not my failing, flailing, and falling flesh.

Want to join me? Let's run flesh free!

Those who live according to the flesh set their minds on the things of the flesh, but those who live according to the Spirit set their minds on the things of the Spirit. For to set the mind on the flesh is death, but to set the mind on the Spirit is life and peace. For the mind that is set on the flesh is hostile to God, for it does not submit to God's law; indeed, it cannot. Those who are in the flesh cannot please God. You, however, are not in the flesh but in the Spirit, if in fact the Spirit of God dwells in you. If you live according to the flesh you will die, but if by the Spirit you put to death the deeds of the body, you will live. For all who are led by the Spirit of God are sons of God. ~ Romans 8:5-9,13-14 ESV

~ More Than... ~

Do you love God more than the emotion of loving God?

Do you love worshiping God more than the feeling you receive from a good worship song?

Do you love God more than you love your possessions, your friends, and your family?

Do you love yourself, your goals and dreams, more than God, His ways, and His purposes?

Do you give up too easily and forget too quickly that God provides more than you could ask or imagine?

Heavenly Father, help me to love You more than anything and place You above everything else in my life. Because You are more than enough for every, need, want, and desire. Thank You for being the God of exceedingly, abundantly, more than we can ask or imagine. Thank You that when I love, serve, and think about You more than anything else, I am free to be more than me.

~ Crawling Out Of The Boat ~

I pray to honor the Lord with all I do, say, and write. Instead my failures rear their ugly heads, and inadequacies whisper words of doubt. Who are you to write? What on earth are you thinking? Knees bent, I plead and grovel. Help me Lord! Send someone to firm up the areas where I'm weak.

Knowledge is growing, but there is still an abundance to learn. I wring my hands, stare at my computer screen, and try not to curl into a ball.

I can't do this alone.

For the umpteenth time I read the verses in Matthew. Peter said to Jesus, "Lord, if it is You, command me to come to You on the water." So He said, "Come." And when Peter had come down out of the boat, he walked on the water to go to Jesus. But when he saw that the wind was boisterous, he was afraid; and beginning to sink he cried out, saying, "Lord, save me!" And immediately Jesus stretched out His hand and caught him, and said to him, "O you of little faith, why did you doubt?" ~ Matthew 14:28-31 NKJV.

I'm so like Peter. I only see what I can't do, not what God can do. For years I've envisioned myself taking that leap of faith. Instead, I tentatively crawl out of the boat donning my life vest, water wings, snorkel, and flippers.

Why do I doubt?

The help I need is found in God—His strength, His power, His might, His sufficiency. I can do all things through Christ who strengthens me. All things, not just some things—all things. I'm taking off the life vest, water wings, snorkel, and flippers, crawling out of the boat and flinging myself straight into the living water of my "all things are possible" God!

I can do all things through Him who strengthens me. ~ Philippians 4:13 NASB

~ Safe In His Hands ~

Have you ever been in a body of water completely panicked, with arms flailing, thinking you're drowning, when in reality all you had to do was lower your feet and stand up?

I've been there, done that. Rather embarrassing, but very comforting when those toes touch sand or terra firma.

Which got me to wondering, how often do we as Christians flounder, flap, and flail in the midst of our circumstances?

How often do we forget Jesus promises no one will ever snatch us from the safety of His hand. Stop, rest, think about, and relish that wonderful truth.

No matter what difficulties we face, we really are always safe in God's hands and firmly planted in His love. And when we take the time to be still, and remember God is in control our flailing stops. *Be still* in Hebrew means to sink down, let drop, be quiet, or relax.

How awesome we can lean back, confident in the palm of God's Hands. We are always held secure in the loving hands of Jesus.

I give them eternal life, and they will never perish, and no one will snatch them out of my hand. My Father, who has given them to me, is greater than all, and no one is able to snatch them out of the Father's hand. ~ John 10:28-29 ESV

~ Perfect Counsel ~

Our college-aged son stopped by my study. Worry seemed to crease his forehead as he sat in the chair across from my desk. I quickly put on my fix-it-all-mom hat and began bestowing sage advice. I was on a roll. Mentally, I was waving my virtual cheerleading pom-poms as I sought to encourage him.

He thanked me and left. Satisfied all was well, I went back to work.

Less than an hour went by before he returned. He confided that during our earlier conversation he had actually been in a great mood, and my quick counsel had done the exact opposite of my intent. I had completely missed the mark.

Ouch. Obviously, my body-language and mind-reading skills were lacking. Fortunately, my son is quick to give grace and forgive his misguided momma.

Have you ever had someone who offered too quick or uninformed advice? Friends and family may fail on comfort or counsel, but God's counsel never misses the mark. I am so grateful Jesus knows precisely what is happening with us every moment of our days. We can be confident when we seek His advice, we will find the exact mercy, grace, and perfect counsel for every need.

Heavenly Father thank You for Your perfect counsel. Help me to stay in Your word so I can soak in Your guidance, and remember to talk to You before I counsel anyone else.

Since then we have a great high priest who has passed through the heavens, Jesus, the Son of God, let us hold fast our confession. For we do not have a high priest who is unable to sympathize with our weaknesses, but one who in every respect has been tempted as we are, yet without sin. Let us then with confidence draw near to the throne of grace, that we may receive mercy and find grace to help in time of need.~ Hebrews 4:14-16 ESV

~ Landmarks ~

Research shows when people are lost, they tend to walk in circles. Our pastor is a former forest ranger. He explained if you are ever lost in a forest, climb a tree or find high ground to get your bearings. Then fix your eyes on one spot before you move forward. To keep from going around in circles, make sure you can always keep your target in focus.

The same is true in life. It's easy to get side-tracked or lost in the forest of busyness, worries, and fears. There are so many distractions every day that spin our lives in circles. We have to remember to keep our eyes fixed on our soul landmark -- Jesus.

In Jesus, the eternal heavenly-based landmark, we find peace. In Him we find direction. In Him we find wisdom, and In Christ we are never, ever lost.

Let us run the race that is before us and never give up. We should remove from our lives anything that would get in the way and the sin that so easily holds us back. Let us look only to Jesus, the One who began our faith and who makes it perfect. ~ Hebrews 12:1-2 NCV.

~ *Flying Or Dragging?* ~

A butterfly struggles to release from the cocoon, but only through the struggle will the wings be squeezed and properly formed to take flight.

Like the Butterfly we want to break free from the pressure and difficulties of our cocoons. However if we don't accept the refining, the adversities of life for ourselves and others, we might have wings, but we will never fly as intended.

We don't want to suffer, and we don't want others to endure hardships. We can choose to fight against our situations and continue to crawl on the ground. We can even come through our cocoon of suffering, but drag the shell of our past behind us and wonder why we can't fly.

Or we can press into God and His word, trust Him that all things work to the good for those who love Him, and we will fly free.

James reminds us, "Consider it a sheer gift, friends, when tests and challenges come at you from all sides. You know that under pressure, your faith-life is forced into the open and shows its true colors. So don't try to get out of anything prematurely. Let it do its work so you become mature and well-developed, not deficient in any way." ~ James 1:2-4 MSG

No more dragging the past, I'm accepting the adversities knowing that God is maturing and perfecting my life so I may fly free.

~ *The Summons* ~

I received a summons notice to be available for Federal jury duty for the entire month of July. Every Friday afternoon, I had to call and check a recorded message to see if I would serve on the following Monday morning.

Scrambling like crazy, I edited my prerecorded shows for Living Joyfully Free, then wrote blog and audio posts and placed them in the queue. Guests waiting to be interviewed were placed on hold until August.

I couldn't plan anything. I had to stop.

The summons came from the court system, but the blessing came from above. God used the interruption to interrupt my hurried and harried schedule. He blessed me by prying me away from the busyness of working on "good" things to focus on the very best – HIM.

I was missing God and missing His blessings. Because of the summons, my focus refocused on God and off what I can do for God. I can breathe again as I paused to breathe in from His Holy Spirit. My ears were unstopped to hear His voice.

God summoned, and my soul answered His call.

How is God summoning you?

I will give you the treasures of darkness, riches stored in secret places, so that you may know that I am the LORD, the God of Israel, who summons you by name. ~ Isaiah 45:3 NIV

~ Poured Out Love ~

ShoShone Falls located in Idaho, towers thirty-six feet higher than Niagara Falls. The sight is amazing. The water flows around a bend in the river, rushes and cascades over several layers of huge, jagged rocks, and drops 212 feet. A spray rises into the sky and at the bottom is a beautiful rainbow.

Standing in the mist, listening to the roar of the water, viewing the beauty and wonder of it all, I visualized God's love pouring down on His children. Romans 5:5 reminds us that God has poured out His love into our hearts. Not just trickling, but gushing, limitless love.

And with that thought, if God is love, why is there suffering? I have friends unable to move from their beds or couches, locked in agonizing pain and various stages of illness. Other friends have suffered terribly at the hands of others. The world is an absolute mess with an abundance of suffering. With human eyes, all I see is water smashing against rocks and the foam of turmoil. I don't see the rainbow at journey's end.

I don't always see the layers that Paul discusses in Romans 5:3-5 that suffering produces perseverance; perseverance, character; and character, hope. And hope does not disappoint.

I can't see the ending—yet. But one day we will be home, and all our tears and all our sorrow will be swept away by the poured out love of our Heavenly Father.

Hold on my friends, life can be a bumpy, wild ride, but hope doesn't disappoint. God is pouring out His love. Not just a tiny misting. We are talking, all out, thundering, awe-inspiring, pain and illness removing, past restoring, sin cleansing, eternal, joy-filled home!

Heavenly Father thank You that one day we'll be home, and Your love will wash away every sorrow and every tear. Let me stay in Your presence where You can pour out Your love on me so I may pour out Your love on others.

~ *Prancing Shoes* ~

Feet shuffling, back hunched, I stood at the sink. I was tired, disappointed, and dragging. Yep, pitiful. And there's nothing quite so pitiful as a pitiful Buffaloe.

As my thoughts trudged through my brain, I felt a nudge in my spirit–was I walking and talking like I believed?

Ouch.

Straightening up, I put a spring back in my step. Because God is able to do immeasurably more than all we ask or imagine according to His power at work within us. And to top it off, He who began a good work in us is faithful to complete it. Nothing is too hard for God, because with Him all things are possible.

Mercy me, I need to get on my prancing shoes and walk and talk believing God's truth!

Heavenly Father Your grace, mercy, and love, makes me dance and prance with joy.

~ Ephesians 3:20, Philippians 1:6, Jeremiah 32:17, Mark 9:23

~ Beyond The Wounds ~

One of my favorite quotes is by St. Augustine "In my deepest wound, I saw Your glory and it dazzled me."

Through my trials, difficulties, detours into sin, I have learned more of God's character, grace, mercy, love, and trustworthiness. They have given me opportunities to better understand who God is and how I fit into His perfect plan.

Does that mean I don't have any moments I'm not hurt, confused, or crawling on wobbly knees? Oh my, some days I feel like I'm swinging on a vine in the jungle and screaming madly.

I haven't liked any of the bad moments, but I wouldn't change them for the world, because I see glimpses of His glory in my wounds.

Whatever you have been through, whatever difficulties you face, God is with you. He will never leave your side and someday, beyond the wounds, you too will see God's glory.

So be truly glad. There is wonderful joy ahead, even though you have to endure many trials for a little while. These trials will show that your faith is genuine. It is being tested as fire tests and purifies gold—though your faith is far more precious than mere gold. So when your faith remains strong through many trials, it will bring you much praise and glory and honor on the day when Jesus Christ is revealed to the whole world. ~ 1 Peter 1:6-7 NLT

~ Faith Leap ~

We all have those little dark closets; the ones sheltering our broken places. The areas someone hurt us, used us, or stole our innocence. Or the areas where we went down the wrong road and hurt not only ourselves but others.

I had a room full of closets. And the doors were tightly bolted, walled behind concrete barriers. In an odd way, I thought ignoring reality worked. Unfortunately, suppressing memories only allowed them to fester or ooze out in strange and unsightly mutations.

They never healed.

With God's gentle nudging, the time finally came for major cleaning. I didn't go quietly. I went kicking and screaming. I hung on for dear life, so afraid if I ventured into the past, I would never return.

I felt like I was being pushed off a thousand foot bridge over a black river filled with hungry crocodiles. Yes I knew God was with me, but I didn't know how far into the deep I would go. What if my tether broke? What if I couldn't come back?

Truth came through God's word that nothing separates us from God's love. Nothing. Not death, life, angels, demons, the present or the future, any powers, height, depth, not anything in creation can separate us from the love of God through Christ Jesus. ~ Romans 8:38-39.

I took the leap, the barriers were removed, and the closets opened. Yes, there were some very painful moments, but God never left my side. And in His love, He provided forgiveness, healing, and restoration.

No matter what we have been through, where our past has carried us, where we are right now at this moment, we will never be separated from the love of God. We can dive without fear, for He is with us, tethered safely to Him for eternity.

When God asks us to return with Him to clean out our past, He's not asking us to bungee jump into the darkness. He's asking us to trust enough to leap into His arms, where we are healed, and fly forever free.

Heavenly Father thank You that I am always safe in Your hands. Help me to trust, believe and leap into the eternal safety of Your love.

~ Finding Your Voice ~

My friends don't talk, think, dress, act, or look alike. Not one is a clone of the other. And I love that!

I love their unique qualities ... from the quirky friend who rattles off one-liners with the speed of a machine gun, to my friend who reads and studies her Bible so much the pages are falling out. The Corinthians went missing for several weeks while she searched for the missing chapter.

Or the girlfriend who gives the best hugs, and the friend who has the gift of organization, and the one who has the gift of hospitality and cooking (neither of which, I might add, are my strong points). I wouldn't want any of my friends to change. I cherish them for who they are.

So how on earth do you find your unique voice?

Be you.

Don't strive to be like someone else. God created you to be you. He loves you just the way you are. Don't compare yourself to others. Allow God to flow through you to use you. Let His words inspire you to share the things He lays on your heart.

You are unique, and therefore your voice is unique. Your voice is a gift straight from God's hands, speak for His glory, and your matchless qualities will touch lives that no one else can touch.

Heavenly Father help me to hear Your voice by reading Your word so that I may use my voice to always speak Your words.

~ *Withered* ~

Ever have one of those days where the winds of life have left you brittle and withered? God's word tells us, blessed is the man who delights in the law of the Lord and on his law he meditates day and night. He is like a tree planted by streams of water, which yields fruit in season and whose leaf doesn't wither. Whatever he does prospers. ~ Psalm 1:1-3.

I wonder ... are we driving our roots deep in His word, or are the winds of adversity blowing the fruit right off our branches? Are we listening to the lies of the devil instead of God's truth? Are we withering up and dying because we aren't allowing God's living water to flow in us and through us?

Dear friends, remember God's truth. Remember His hope. Remember His love. Remember to love The One who loves you with an unfailing love. Refresh yourself in the living water and delight in God's word and watch those withered branches return to vibrant life! ~ John 13:35, Matthew 7:16-20, John 7:38, Revelation 2:3-4

~ Contact ~

First Name: _____
Last Name: _____
Email: _____
Comments: _____

When someone wants to contact me through my website, I have a page where my visitors can send me a note. Unfortunately I didn't realize the page wasn't working correctly. Something was blocking the page from submitting. After an hour of tweaks and manipulation, I was able to correct the problem.

The difficulty made me so grateful God's contact page is never down or not working. He promises, He will hear when we call. He's near to all who call on Him in truth. He says to call Him and He will answer and tell us great and unsearchable things we didn't know ~ Psalm 4:3, 145:18, Jeremiah 33:3.

But there is a warning, sin has separated you from your God; your sins have hidden His face from you, so that He won't hear ~ Isaiah 59:2.

Dear friends remember, the only thing that can block us from God … is us.

Heavenly Father I don't want anything to keep me from contacting You. Let me be quick to ask for forgiveness for any sin and anything that might block me from You.

~ Beyond Limited Vision ~

I'm terribly near-sighted. Without my glasses or contacts, the world is a blur. I can't see two feet in front of my face. Getting behind the wheel of an automobile would be disastrous. For my safety and everyone on the road, I would never drive without corrective lenses.

I wonder how often we go through life confining ourselves and God to only our limited vision. We can "see" our past and see the present, and therefore we don't want to venture outside the comforts of knowing what we know, and seeing what we see.

However if we don't look beyond our past and our daily circumstances, will we miss God's vision?

The amplified version of Proverbs 29:18 says, "Where there is no vision [no redemptive revelation of God], the people perish; but he who keeps the law [of God, which includes that of man]—blessed (happy, fortunate, and enviable) is he."

Our God is the creator of the universe. Think about that. God is the Creator. Of. The. Universe. Nothing is impossible for Him. He is not constrained by time or place. He is omnipresent. Omnipotent. Almighty. God is the God who sees. Things which eye has not seen and ear has not heard, and which have not entered the heart of man, all that God has prepared for those who love Him~ 1 Corinthians 2:9 NASB. God is beyond our limited vision.

Heavenly Father help me to never limit the vision You have for me, open my spiritual eyes to be open to Your unlimited, perfect plans.

~ *Blackmailed* ~

You know "those" things, the times we willingly strayed off God's pathway and engaged in enemy activity we knew was wrong? We didn't just step our toes in the mud, we went head first, and wallowed in the pig-sty of sin. I've been there, done that. Not satisfied with God's best, I've traveled down the wrong roads. I ignored warning signs and headed over the cliff. Sin collisions always results in wreckage, and out of the debris crawls regret, guilt, and condemnation.

Satan, instigator and deceiver, sets us up to fall, or sets us up for abuse, then stands by with virtual camera in hand to capture images. He whispers, shouts, and screams our failures or blames us for what he started in the first place. The enemy is right there to rub our noses in the mess and blackmail us into ineffectiveness in Christ's Kingdom.

If I'm not careful, the dreaded pity party comes to call, complete with an abundance of whine, maybe I'll even put on a sad song so the tears flow freely. "Poor me" I say in my best whiney voice ... "please pass the chocolate." As tempting as it may be to wallow in the muck of the past, there are choices.

Oswald Chambers advised to "take ourselves by the scruff of the neck and shake ourselves" out of our moods. Goodness knows there are days I need a good shaking. We should take every thought captive, but the problem comes when we believe Satan's lie that we deserve to endlessly suffer. We have a choice as to whether those past wounds are medals for the enemy, or medals for Christ's healing and restoration.

God grants us weapons, gives us a battle plan, warns us of enemy attacks, and shows us how we can defend ourselves. We don't have to live in the stench; there are methods for stink removal. Isaiah 43:18-19 tells us to forget the past, don't dwell on them but to watch how God is doing new things.

God blesses us with new mercies and opportunities. His mercies are new every morning. What's done is done, but what is to come through our Savior, is new, vibrant, and exciting. Jesus—the way, the truth, and the life, Prince of Peace, Lord of Lords—rescues us from sin, the pain of yesterday, and gives hope for tomorrow.

Next time the blackmailer comes to call, remind him that there is nothing in your past that hasn't been forgiven, restored, and redeemed by the grace of Jesus Christ.

The steadfast love of the Lord never ceases; his mercies never come to an end; they are new every morning; great is your faithfulness. ~ Lamentations 3:22-23 ESV

~ Incredible You ~

God longs to connect with us. He pursues us. Like the story of the Prodigal son, He runs to us longing to show compassion and mercy. His eyes roam throughout the earth looking for those whose hearts are devoted to Him. He thinks about you day and night.

After thirty-plus moves and various travels, I encounter people who look or act similar to someone I've known in the past. No matter how close their appearance or personality, there are always differences, no one can replace friends I've left behind or those who have gone to be with the Lord. I'll always miss them.

Each of us are uniquely designed by God, and because of that uniqueness there is an ache, a longing, a crevice in our souls nothing and no person can satisfy – except God.

God has that same longing, that same desire to spend time with us. No one else takes your place in His heart. Our hearts are entwined with His and when we spend time with Him, we both find fulfillment.

All around us and inside us we see glimpses of His glory. God sky paints His love in rainbow hues during sunrises and sunsets. His smile is seen in the innocence of a child, the wag of a puppy, or in the purr of a kitten. God's creativity emerges in every plant, bud, and flower. All things are designed with the intricacies of a loving Creator.

And you—incredible you—were lovingly fashioned and formed. Before you were born, and even before you were formed in the womb, God knew you. Regardless of the details of your birth, you were not an accident, you were wanted and planned.

God loves you special because you were created special; heavenly designed by your loving heavenly Father. God created us in His image.

But when we are birthed into this sinful world, no matter how "good" we are, we are stained and tainted. No matter how we scrub ourselves with good works, good thoughts, or good things, nothing can remove life's messes. But when we allow Jesus in our lives we get that scrubbing from the inside out.

And as Christians, we don't lose our identity. God didn't create you to be like anyone else … you don't have to think, act, feel, or be anyone but you. You were placed on planet earth at a specific time for a specific purpose.

And with God's touch we fulfill a plan set out from the foundation of this world. You are lovingly created and designed for love.

Through Christ's presence, we become the absolute best we were designed to be. We don't lose ourselves—we are perfectly loved reflecting perfect love.

Heavenly Father thank You for making me. Help me to see myself through Your loving eyes.

~ *Liquid Love*~

I'm a visual person. I love to sit on the edge of the river and clear out areas that have become stagnant. With each moment of success, each area cleaned, I'm reminded of God's free-flowing love.

My sweet friend, Teena Goble, describes God's love as liquid love—love that pours into every nook and cranny of our lives. God's love is pure, infusing, total, and complete. His love flows like streams in a desert. There is no area too barren or damaged for the touch of God's love.

The Bible tells us God's Love is ... faithful, just, righteous, merciful, abounding in love, great, everlasting to everlasting, gracious, compassionate, slow to anger, rich, covenant of love, endures forever, love that makes deserts bloom, love reaching higher than the heavens, living water love. The love of Christ is wide, long, high, and deep, flooding the soul with unfailing joy. How grateful I am there is no area too dark in our lives that can't be washed clean by Jesus' grace and mercy.

Dive into the living water of God's liquid love.

Heavenly Father, thank You for Your living water that hydrates my soul with Your liquid love.

He who believes in Me [who cleaves to and trusts in and relies on Me] as the Scripture has said, From his innermost being shall flow [continuously] springs and rivers of living water. ~ John 7:38 AMP

~ Dirty Glasses ~

My eyesight is pitiful. I'm a level up from being declared legally blind. Without corrective lenses the world is an interesting blur.

My glasses or contacts, brings the world into focus. However, I want to experience more than corrective eyesight. I want corrective heart and soul sight. I want to see things from a heavenly perspective. An earthly perspective leads to frustration, anger, disappointment, disillusionment, and hopelessness, because we look to people and the things of this world for fulfillment.

We can't look to this world to fix the things of this world — that's like looking through a pair of dirty, slimy glasses hoping to find clarity.

We need to remember as followers of Christ that we are seated in the heavenly realms where all things are revealed and visible. We can "see" beyond our earthly life. Everything doesn't revolve around our existence. There is a huge, amazing reality and inner-working of all things working for the good of those who love the Lord and are called according to His purpose.

Christ is our peace. Christ is our hope. Christ is our freedom. Christ is life. And the reality is, with Christ, and In Christ, whatever happens we are soul safe and will always receive a heavenly happy ending.

Heavenly Father, I want to see life from a heavenly perspective. When I am burdened, help me to cast my cares on You. When I am anxious, remind me that in You I find peace. When life's problems seem so big, turn the eyes of my soul upward to the immense heavens and the enormity of You and Your unfailing love. For with You, all things are possible. And You know the plans You have for each of us, and Your plans are good. Keep my soul-sight smudge free and focused on You!

~ *Perspective* ~

According to NASA, Scientists estimate there are more than 100 billion galaxies scattered throughout the visible universe. The Milky Way is a huge city of stars, so big that even at the speed of light it would take 100,000 years to travel across.

Worry often looms like a huge obstacle. When anxiety creeps up and sends me reeling, I need to remember that the same God who created the infinite universe, names every star, knows every sparrow that falls, and counts the numbers of hair on my head, is big enough to handle any problem or obstacle.

May I share a visual? My sweet hubby and I drove up the nearby mountains to enjoy the beauty. We stopped by the side of the road and I made a snowman and a snow angel.

Are you impressed? Don't be.

My big, fat snowman was only about six inches tall, and my snow angel I made with my fingers.

Perspective.

Life is about perspective.

Dear Heavenly Father, help me to keep my focus on You – incredible, awesome, wonderful, Holy, marvelous, matchless, magnificent, all-knowing, loving, all-powerful, infinite, merciful, righteous, mighty You!

~ *Stopping to Listen* ~

The day gets so busy sometimes. We hit the ground running, and even though we want to spend time with God, we know He's always there.

I was thinking about the verse that says do not grieve the Holy Spirit ... Do not grieve the Holy Spirit of God [do not offend or vex or sadden Him], by Whom you were sealed (marked, branded as God's own, secured) for the day of redemption (of final deliverance through Christ from evil and the consequences of sin) ~ Ephesians 4:30 AMP.

Do you ever think about God being sad?

During my busy morning, I felt like I needed to stop. Really stop. And spend time with God.

And I didn't.

I haven't.

Think about how we feel when we've gone out of our way to try and talk to someone because we have something on our heart to share. But they're distracted and only semi-listening. And we leave and go away sad.

Have you felt that little tug, or a gentle nudge to spend time reading the Bible or praying, and instead ignored the feeling? Did you realize we are actually ignoring a request from God? And then we wonder why we don't feel connected with Him.

I don't want to sadden God's heart. I want Him to know I love Him. And the best way I can show God I love Him is by spending time with Him. So I'm going to get on my knees. And I'm going to talk to The One who wants to hear my voice.

He wants to hear from you too.

Spend time with Him. Right now. He's calling. He loves you, He wants to spend time with you. He wants to hear your voice. And He wants you to know you are eternally loved.

Heavenly Father my soul kneels in Your presence. My heart is open to You.

~ *In Love!* ~

When I was dating my husband, Dennis, people ran the other way when they saw me coming. They were sick of hearing how wonderful I thought he was -- how cute, smart, funny, handsome, etc. I could not wait to see, talk to, and spend time with him. Why? I was in love. Not in love, but IN LOVE! The kind where you walk a few feet off the ground, the birds sing special songs, sunsets are brighter, and all is right with the world.

I could have read books on Dennis, such as *The proper care and feeding of a Buffaloe, The Buffaloe whisperer,* and *Twenty-One helpful tips on dating a Buffaloe.* I could have talked to other people who knew him, sang songs about him, *Oh give me a home where the Buffaloe roam...*

However until I spent time with him one-on-one, I didn't have a personal relationship nor personal knowledge. The more we discovered about one another, the deeper our love grew. A loving relationship is two-sided, built on communication to know and be known.

God also wants you to experience an intimate connection with Him. God already knows you and everything about you, but in discovering and knowing Him, we find who He is and who *we* are created to be.

I've seen people literally cringe when someone mentioned God spoke to them. I've done the same thing. It seems rather presumptuous to think that God of would audibly speak to someone other than a Biblical hero. Thankfully references are throughout the Bible on everyday people hearing and listening to God. Movies have tried to capture this concept using different methods ranging from a booming voice from the sky to some rather interesting actor portrayals.

The amazing fact remains, God really does want to communicate with each of us. Prayer isn't intended as a monologue but a dialogue.

When our son was three, he practically talked nonstop. No matter where he was or what he was doing, he talked. And when he talked, he asked questions to make sure I was listening. By the time he was finally in bed, I thought my ears would melt off my head. One afternoon after a rather verbose day, I slumped to the top of the stairs and crashed on the floor.

He didn't even notice I wasn't still in the room. He continued to talk. An hour passed and he still talked. Finally there was a moment of silence.

"Mom?"

"I'm up here."I answered.

Without a moment's hesitation he continued talking. He just needed to know I was still close enough to hear. I also need that connection with God. I want to know He listens and He hears when I call. However there is more to prayer than just throwing our requests up to heaven. We actually do need to listen.

God is in-love with you, longs to hear your voice, and spend time with you. God's love longs to whisper in your soul how much He loves you.

Heavenly Father, I love You. I'm so amazed You love me. Help me to still my soul to listen for Your voice whispering in my spirit.

~ Hearts Afire ~

They said to one another, 'Were not our hearts burning within us while He was speaking to us on the road, while He was explaining the Scriptures to us? ~ Luke 24:32 NAS

When I lived in Texas my friend, Rita, and I would walk for exercise. Most days our pace was brisk as we discussed God and His word. However, the days we were sidetracked on an issue or concern, the walk seemed hard and long.

What was the difference? The road and scenery were the same but our hearts were different. When we spoke of God and His word, the time flew and our speed quickened.

Luke 24, records the story of two men who walked with heavy hearts on the road to Emmaus as they discussed Jesus' crucifixion earlier in the week. Discouragement, despair, and sadness permeated the air as their feet shuffled along the rocky road. How they hoped Jesus would have been the one to redeem and set Israel free.

A stranger joined them and asked about their conversation. They were amazed anyone would not know the events surrounding Jesus and His death. Then the stranger stated the scriptural prophecies beginning with Moses to their present time about Jesus. Their pace quickened, and their minds raced as they traveled along the road.

Their journey ended and they begged the stranger to stay with them. He agreed and reclined at the table to eat. When the bread was broken, their eyes were opened and they recognized the stranger as the risen Lord, Jesus Christ. As quickly as Jesus appeared, He was gone, but one thing remained—their burning hearts.

As a young man, Jim Elliot felt the call of God on his heart. He wrote in his diary in the summer of 1947, "He makes His ministers a flame of fire. Am I ignitable? God deliver me from the dread of asbestos of 'other things.' Saturate me with the oil of the Spirit that I may be a flame. But flame is transient, often short-lived. Canst thou bear this, my soul--short life? In me there dwells the Spirit of the Great Short-Lived, whose zeal for God's house consumed Him. 'Make me Thy Fuel, Flame of God.'"*

Jim Elliot become a missionary and was martyred by the very people he had ventured to save. Yet his testimony sparked a major revival in the hearts of missionaries worldwide. Jim's words from the past challenge me to ignite my soul for God.

We too can keep our heart-flames burning bright through prayer and by reading God's word.

Heavenly Father, help me to walk in Your way. Keep my heart burning with Your truth and Your way. Make me Your fuel, flame of God.

*Elizabeth Elliot, *Through Gates of Splendor*, Tyndale House Publishers, Carol Stream, IL, p 6.

~ Feeling Connected ~

I've had times when I've felt out of touch with God. I've begged and pleaded for forgiveness if sin is an issue, read the Bible looking for answers, and fallen on my knees searching for His presence.

I would prefer to live on a spiritual mountaintop. I want the emotion, that natural "high" when the connection between child and Heavenly Father seem strongest. I know God is there, but I want to feel Him. Unfortunately life has to be lived in the day-to-day mundane existence, where trials and troubles exist, and emotions are carried like the wind. I can't trust only what I "feel." I must trust what I know is true.

During my fight against Lyme disease, the doctors at three separate times put me on intravenous antibiotics. To start the process, I traveled to the hospital to receive a PICC line. (The PICC line is a small catheter inserted into a peripheral vein on the inside of the arm about three to six inches from the elbow. The line runs through the vein to the superior vena cava or the right atrium of the heart.) The process is not fun, they don't put you to sleep or give you a shot—thank the Lord for Lidocaine.

The doctor would supply a week's worth of saline, heparin shots, and self-deflating antibiotic balls for home administration. Every eight hours one medicine ball would be removed and another attached. At 4:45 each morning, the now deflated medicine ball would be removed, my PICC line flushed with saline and heparin, and a new ball reattached.

The first few minutes the medicine would still be cool, and I could feel it running through the vein. After about five minutes, the fluid would be the same temperature as my blood and would no longer be felt. Yet I could watch the ball slowly deflate, and know without a doubt the medicine was being delivered.

Even when we can't feel God, we can be assured His love is constantly pouring into our lives through His Holy Spirit. He is always near. His word promises, the closer we draw to God, the more we seek His presence, the more we find a deep, intimate, loving relationship. Not religion, or rote memorization, but a vibrant free-flowing, intimate, friendship.

Heavenly Father thank You that Your love always flows free.

~ Resurrection ~

A friend died, and I cried so much the corner of my eyes peeled. I was totally drained, almost hollow inside. God never left me for a moment, but I felt removed and couldn't feel His presence. I couldn't sleep, and I was desperate to find my way back to Him. I begged Him to find me, needed His touch to pull me back.

Emotions are fickle and toss and blow with the wind of circumstances. I must remember God never changes. He is always there and always love. Even during the times I feel alone, He is always near and ever-present. So I cry out to Him, take the pieces in Your hand and make me whole again.

And slowly I open my heart once again as winter thaws in my heart and through His comfort I sense the buds of spring.

Dear one, you are never, ever alone. God is The God of resurrection. Winter will turn to Spring and with His touch comes beauty even in the midst of suffering. Stretch out your hands to Him, He waits to provide comfort.

Take heart dear one. Suffering comes, but My comfort will overflow to you. ~ 2 Corinthians 1:5

~ Captivating Thoughts ~

We all have them. Those thoughts that awaken us in the night or make us cringe in the light of day. They usually come out of thin air, at the worst times, and send our minds whirling.

2 Corinthians 10:5 advises us to demolish arguments and every pretension that sets itself up against the knowledge of God, and take captive every thought to make it obedient to Christ. However, once we take them prisoner, what do we do with them? They continue to torment us from behind their jail bars.

For decades the enemy kept me silent and locked tight in a lie. For those of you who know my past, some bad things happened. And during those moments of trauma, my throat would close and I could not scream. The enemy planted a lie that if I ever told anyone he would again attack.

I lived in that terror for most of my life.

The time finally came to give voice to my fear and place it completely in God's hands. So out came the lie. I voiced it, stood it up in front of my prayer group, and we prayed to see God's truth. Because anything the enemy wants you to keep in the darkness and hidden, needs to be taken before God's light.

Taking thoughts captive isn't just about shoving them behind bars; it is exploring God's truth and finding the reality of God's might, power, forgiveness, mercy, and grace. Total freedom comes from, and in, God's truth.

Knowing (truly knowing) God's word demolishes the lies and bad thoughts. The sword of the Spirit cuts off the enemy's lies. Jesus said, if you hold to my teaching, you are really my disciples. Then you will know the truth, and the truth will set you free. For I will give you utterance and wisdom which none of your opponents will be able to resist or refute ~ John 8:31-32, Luke 21:15.

Pray, study, and learn, ask God to send forth His light and truth to guide you ~ Psalm 43:3. Take every thought captive, wrap it in God's truth, throw it out, smash it, destroy it, and live free. For, greater is our God than the one who is in the world ~ 1 John 4:4.

My voice is back. I can scream, but better than that, I can shout victory! Let's wield our sword of the Spirit, and smash, demolish, and force those lies and bad thoughts to succumb to the power of our Most High God and mighty Savior.

Heavenly Father thank You that with You we can take thoughts captive and in You we are always victorious.

~ *Prayer Revolutionaries* ~

During World War II, the 6th Ranger Battalion, assisted by Filipino guerrillas, penetrated deep into enemy territory to free prisoners of war at Cabanatuan. One of the primary concerns was the flatness of the countryside. The terrain had been cleared of vegetation. The Rangers would have to crawl through a long, open field on their bellies, right under the eyes of the guards. They would only have an hour of full darkness as the sun set below the horizon and the moon rose.

As a distraction, a P-61 Black Widow flew over the prison camp. The pilot cut the power to the left engine at 1,500 feet, restarted it, creating a loud backfire, and repeated the procedure twice more, losing altitude to 200 feet. Pretending the plane was crippled, the pilot headed toward low hills, clearing them by a mere thirty feet.

The ruse continued for twenty minutes, creating a diversion for the Rangers inching their way toward the camp on their bellies. After crawling more than a mile, the soldiers attacked the prison and freed 500 POWs.

Reading this amazing story I wonder, where are today's spiritual soldiers? Are we willing to spend time in the heavenlies for spiritual cover to assist those battling on the front lines? Are we willing to crawl forward into enemy territory?

The need is great. The workers are few.

Oh but what amazing rewards await those who enlist in God's army. Prison doors are opened, chains fall away, and captives are set free. The battles rage, but victory is eminent, because all things are possible with God.

Let's get on our knees and raid the enemy's POW camps!

The prayer of a righteous man is powerful and effective. ~ James 5:16

~ Deliverance ~

We want God's deliverance. We want God to deliver when we want Him to deliver – *before* the pain and *before* the suffering.

However, Joseph was sold into slavery, falsely accused, and spent years in prison. Shadrach, Meshach, and Abednego were thrown in a blazing fire. Daniel was tossed to hungry lions. Paul and Silas were beaten and chained in a dungeon. Early Christians were persecuted, tortured, and sent fleeing throughout the known world. Jesus was beaten and died on a cross.

God's deliverance is life and resurrection in the midst of pain, suffering, and death. Deliverance comes in the fire, in the midst of lions, in the dark-dingy jail cells, and in persecution. Deliverance leads to nations being spared, rulers discovering The true God, jailers receiving new life, and the gospel being spread throughout the world.

Heavenly Father help me to see beyond my limited earthly vision to Your greater purpose. Help me to always remember You are my deliverer, and the ultimate deliverance came in Jesus' sacrifice and resurrection. Deliver me to You, so I may be used for Your purposes to share Your eternal deliverance.

~ Genesis 37, Genesis 39-47, Daniel 3, Daniel 6, Acts 16, John 19-21, Acts 8:1-4, Hebrews 11

~ No One Could Love You More ~

To live free and beyond our circumstances, we need to understand and believe our Heavenly Father loves us. Take a break from your struggles, lay them down, seek God's presence instead of worrying about the past, today, or the future.

Remove the veil of problems and worries. Think and meditate on God. Don't look for answers, look for Him. Praise Him, count your blessings, look, ask, and expect. Pray.

When talking to God tonight, remove the distractions. Whatever occupies our mind becomes an idol. Concentrating, meditating on God and His loving character turns us away from ourselves, and our problems, and back to Him.

Walls and barriers are erected around our hearts that keep us from intimacy with God and with others. Let down the walls, crawl over, come sit with God (visualize your favorite place-- on the porch, at the ocean, in the mountains).

Enjoy God, because in His presence is fullness of joy. Focus on what is good, right, and acceptable. Remember His every good and perfect gift – His wonderful nature, the smile of a friend, the belly laugh of a toddler, the wag of a puppy, the purr of a kitten.

Beth Moore shared on one of her trips that she danced a ballet for God in her hotel room. When have you danced a ballet before God?

God tells us to come to Him like little children. Skip with God. When is the last time you played? Praise Him. Praise drives away our problems. There is no set way, no formula for your prayer time, allow God to lead.

We can't grow, won't trust, and won't believe God, if we don't drive down deep within our souls the realization that God truly is love and has our best interest at heart.

Jesus willingly came from glory, lived on this dusty earth for thirty three years, was beaten and tortured and died on the cross for you. And then when all sin was paid, all penalty completed, He rose from the grave to make a way for you to be in relationship with a Holy God. No one could ever love you more.

Heavenly Father thank You for Your joyful, ever-present love.

~ Healing Layers ~

My past is riddled with shattered places, dark places and memories I hoped to forever ignore. The Band-Aid applications I tried on my own, couldn't clean the old wounds, they continued to fester. God's indwelling Spirit ever gently, so gently, prodded me forward to allow God full access to His healing. I wrestled and fought, worried that if I unlocked the past, I would drown in horrifying memories and never return.

One night I dreamt Jesus held my hand and walked with me through my past. And as we walked, He showed how He loved and cared for me through the moments of abuse, and how His presence heals all wounds. The process was painful and scary, but only because of my own unfounded fears.

God is a good Father; He removes the monsters hiding under the bed, the ones in the closets, and the terrors that crouch in the dark rooms. And as God tenderly pulls away layers concealed in the shadows, His light cleanses, renews, and brings wonderful freedom. Because there is no memory too dark, no sin too hidden, and no abuse too great for the healing touch of God.

Thank You Heavenly Father that You heal the brokenhearted and bind up all wounds. Thank You that nothing in our past is too dark for the cleansing of Your gentle, healing light.

~ The Race ~

In the Barcelona, Spain 1992 Olympics, Derek Redmond was touted as one of the best. His awards were many and included World Silver and Gold Medals in the 400m and 4 x 400m competitions. He had trained and prepared for the 1992 Olympics. He knew the risks. As an athlete in the 1988 Olympics an Achilles tendon injury forced him to withdraw only a few moments before the race.

Four years and five surgeries later, he was determined to medal in the 400. Barcelona would be his opportunity. No matter what, he would finish strong. During each qualifying race, Derek ran well, recording the fastest time of the first round and winning his quarter-final heat.

Jim Redmond, his father watched in anticipation as Derek settled into the starting blocks for the semi-finals. Derek got off to a clean start and quickly took the lead. His win looked imminent. Then the unthinkable happened. With a pop Derek's right hamstring muscle tore and he fell to the ground in agony.

Jim, seeing his son in trouble raced from the top row of the stands.

Determined to finish, Derek lifted himself to his feet, his leg quivering, and ever so slowly, hobbled down the track, waving away the oncoming medical personnel. He limped onward, his tear-stained face twisted in agony. The race now over, the crowd of 65,000 rose to their feet and cheer. The volume grew as Redmond, in searing pain took one painful step at a time.

His father finally reached the bottom of the stands, leapt over the railing, and with two security officers chasing after him, ran to help.

"I'm here, son," Jim hugged his son. "We'll finish together."

Sobbing, Derek placed his arm around his father's shoulders.

Arm in arm, they continued their painful journey. Just before the finish, Jim released Derek. He completed the course on his own. The crowd in total frenzy responded with a standing ovation.

With tears in his eyes, Jim Redmond told the press afterwards. "I'm the proudest father alive. I'm prouder of him than I would have been if he had won the gold medal."

Derek Redmond's name will be remembered long after records are broken and medals tarnish. He persevered, and with his father's help, finished strong.

God is our ever-present help. He will never leave or forsake you. He will hold you close through every step of your journey and welcome you home as you cross the final finish line.

~ *Trash To Treasure* ~

Nestled in Fort Worth's Botanical Gardens, The Japanese Gardens are a tranquil retreat from the rush of the world. The beautiful plants mesh with the gentle, rolling terrain, making it seem that the gardens have existed for hundreds of years. Exotic Imperial Koi unafraid of humans beg for food pellets dispensed to visitors for a quarter. Squirrels, turtles, lizards, ducks, and geckos run freely. Trees sway in the gentle breeze and water skips across the rocks of waterfalls.

My family visited the site for years before learning the land was originally a gullied bluff used as a watering hole for cattle, a trash dump, a squatter's camp, and then as a gravel pit to build the streets of old Fort Worth.

Never would we have guessed something so beautiful could have come from such an ugly beginning.

How many stood over the trash heap of a life and declared that it would always be a trash heap?

God sees beyond the gravel, the trash, the squatters of sin, despair, and hopelessness, He cleans us up and then provides a place of beauty for us and others. 2 Corinthians 5:17 reminds us if we are in Christ we are new creations.

God's forgiveness changes lives. We can trust Him with our past. We can trust Him to forgive, and when we do He renews our lives and recreates us into walking testaments of His grace and mercy.

Look, I am about to do something new; even now it is coming. Do you not see it? Indeed, I will make a way in the wilderness, rivers in the desert. ~ Isaiah 43:19 HCSB

~ The Rest Of The Story ~

Sometimes life doesn't seem fair and horrible things happen. But here on earth we can only see a small part, like picking up a book, reading the first few pages, but never discovering the positive ending.

I have scars to prove my difficulties, yet I can personally attest how God heals and mends every torn and broken place. And how every moment of heartache and pain has been restored and used for good purposes.

When I write difficult scenes for my novels, I've found myself crying and praying for my fictional characters. I hate to see someone suffer even if it is only on paper. The situations I put my characters through may not seem fair at the time, but I know everything will be okay. I know the difficulty will make them stronger and help others. I can see the finished product. I know the ending.

God knows your full and complete story. He knows each page and chapter of your life. Not one minute of your life is wasted. And if you are in Christ, the ending always comes with a happily-ever-after.

Heavenly Father thank You for happy endings. Thank You that You are always in control and You have bigger purposes than we can imagine. I look forward to reading the rest of the story when I am safe forever in Your arms.

~ Truth And Consequences ~

When Jesus was accosted in the Garden of Gethsemane by a crowd armed with swords and clubs, His disciples scattered and hid. They cowered in fear. Peter denied Jesus three times. Yet, a few days later these same men spoke boldly testifying to seeing Jesus alive. They stood firm preaching that Jesus had been raised from the dead. Women testified seeing and conversing with Jesus. Five hundred people witnessed Jesus alive, and He appeared over a period of forty days before ascending into Heaven.

How did a rag-tag group of followers all of the sudden become bold enough to speak to those who had just crucified Jesus? How did they go from fear to incredible confidence? Why did they willingly endure imprisonments, beatings, torture, and horrible deaths?

Because they knew, they believed, they witnessed, and they experienced Jesus.

I am a Christ follower. I believe Jesus Christ is the Son of God. I believe He was beaten and crucified on a cross for our sins. I believe He died and rose again on the third day, defeating death and opening a path for forgiveness, mercy, and fellowship with God. I don't worship an idol, object, idea, thought, church, or antiquity; I worship the risen Lord, Jesus Christ. I've given my heart, body, soul, and mind to Christ Jesus. His Spirit dwells within me. My belief is not based on a feeling or an emotion, but based on fact. I know whom I have believed.

You too can know and experience Jesus. He died and rose again for you—to give you an opportunity to be forgiven and have a relationship with God. Good works, church membership, denominations, religiosity, good family history, etc. won't get you into Heaven. Even saying you believe in God isn't enough. The Bible says, you believe there is one God. Good! Even the demons believe that—and shudder ~ James 2:19. Even the demons believe God exists.

So what do you do? Jesus is the way, the truth, and the life.

The apostle Paul put it pretty plainly, If you confess with your mouth, 'Jesus is Lord,' and believe in your heart God raised him from the dead, you will be saved. For it is with your heart you believe and are justified, and it is with your mouth that you confess and are saved ~ Romans 10:9-10. And when you believe, when you accept Jesus into your heart, your life will never be the same.

Christianity (following Christ) is not a list of rules to follow, but freedom to live life fully in tune with our awesome God. Fear is replaced with confidence. Cowardice is replaced with boldness. And you are given a new life—new, eternal, restored, renewed, recreated life in Jesus Christ.

The truth and consequences of the resurrection is eternal. Will you believe?

Remember, whatever you believe has eternal consequences.

~ Matthew 26:36-75, Matthew 28:1-10, John 8:34-36, John 14: 6, Acts 1:1-11, Acts 2:14-2, Acts 4:1-21, 1 Corinthians 15:3-8, 2 Corinthians 3:17-18.

~ But God ~

Sin interrupts our ability to connect with God. I know. There were times sin presented itself as an ocean of delight, and I would think perhaps I could just put my toe into the edge of the water and no one would get hurt. Unfortunately that toe led to full immersion and I would be horrified as I plunged deep into the muddy water. Than I'd hide from God until I couldn't take the separation any longer. And I would run to Him begging for His grace.

Thankfully regardless of our past, no matter what has happened, what we have been through, God's forgiveness and healing are available.

At the 2004 Athens Olympics, 14 year old, South Korean swimmer Park Tae-Hwan fell into the pool just before the starting buzzer sounded for his preliminary round in the Men's 400m Freestyle. He was disqualified and fled to the bathroom to hide his shame.

Four years later at Beijing, his nerves steadier, the 18-year-old won the gold medal in the same event, and claimed his country's first-ever Olympic swimming medal.

What if Park had allowed himself to continue in his despair and relied on his momentary feelings -- fallen, ashamed, heartbroken, not worthy of ever trying again?

In our own lives, failures are replayed in our minds or others won't allow us to move on and forget. But God is a compassionate, forgiving God.

David was an adulterer and murderer, but God called him a man after His own heart. Moses killed a man, but God spoke to him face-to-face as a friend. Rahab was a prostitute, but God blessed her to be in the lineage of Jesus Christ. Paul was present and perhaps authorized the stoning of Steven and also persecuted Christians, but God used Paul in mighty ways to further His kingdom.

The Bible is full of examples with imperfect people—prostitutes, liars, adulterers, murderers, and thieves. All of them were accepted and made whole through God's grace, mercy, and forgiveness.

God redeems and restores lives. Forgiveness is a Holy God reaching through the outstretched hands of His precious son Jesus, where all our sins were nailed to the cross. We would all be lost, but for the grace of God.

But God showed his great love for us by sending Christ to die for us while we were still sinners. ~ Romans 5:8 NLT

~ *Rimmer* ~

One of my friend's childhood home resided over the bar owned by her parents. She called herself a "rimmer" because she grew up on the "toilet rim of life." She called me a "lifer" because I had spent my life growing up in the church. As our friendship grew, she confided something she had never shared with anyone. Some people in the church would never forgive her if they knew. Some wouldn't want them walking in their doors. But because of God's grace and mercy I knew God forgave her, I knew her heart, and I know God's heart. God is a forgiving God.

Think what you would term an unforgivable sin.

Thankfully, God's grace isn't limited by our earthly thinking. Only God is a righteous judge. God forgives us, and we can trust Him to do what is right when we forgive others. It's far too easy to point fingers at someone else's sins. We are too quick to throw stones at sins we don't think we commit. It's so easy to quote, 1 Corinthians 6:9-10 that the sexually immoral, idolaters, adulterers, male prostitutes, homosexual offenders, thieves, the greedy, the drunkards, slanderers, and swindlers won't inherit the kingdom of God.

But what wonderful hope and encouragement are found in the next verse. And that is what some of you were. But you were washed, you were sanctified, you were justified in the name of the Lord Jesus Christ and by the Spirit of our God, 1 Corinthians 6:11. Perhaps your sins don't seem "that" major, or categorized as one of "*those* sins."

Remember, only one sin—one lie, one tiny "white" lie, one small theft, one note of gossip, one lingering unwholesome look at another, one moment of pride, one unkind word, one wicked thought or action, one sinful thought—only one sin will keep you from standing in front of a Holy God.

Not one of us is perfect. Not one of us is without sin. God doesn't grade on the curve. Without grace I would be toast — burnt toast. For all have sinned and fall short of the glory of God ~ Romans 3:23.

Thankfully, God loved the world enough to send His Son so that anyone who believes in Him will have eternal life. God didn't send His Son to condemn the world but to save the world ~ John 3:16-17. Jesus holds out nail-scarred hands of redemption, grace, and mercy.

We were once broken, once lost, once sinners, now forgiven and made whole. Regardless of what *we were,* Christ offers forgiveness, freedom, renewal, restoration, and life eternal.

Grace. God's Grace. *Amazing* Grace.

~ Why Won't You Trust Me? ~

My love never fails. My promises never fail. My strength, might, and power are more powerful than any other strength, might, or power. My desire is that none should perish. My forgiveness forgives in abundance. My grace is sufficient. My presence is with you. My Word will guide you. My wisdom shouts wisdom to the listening ear. My ears hear your call. My goals and plans are for your best. My paths are the best paths. My Spirit intercedes for you. My hands reach out to you. My Word is truth. My peace and joy are available for you. My possibilities are beyond any impossibility. My unfailing love for you, and my life which I've given for you, lasts through eternity.

Why won't you trust Me?

Will you trust *Me*?

Blessed is the man who trusts in the LORD, whose trust is the LORD. ~ *Jeremiah 17:7 ESV*

~ Something Stinketh ~

A strange odor seeped from our refrigerator. You know the smell is bad when a teenage boy thinks it's disgusting.

After putting on my Hazmat suit, gas mask and rubber gloves, I removed strange mutations growing in the vegetable drawer. I cleaned bins and wiped shelves until everything sparkled and the fridge smelled great.

Ignoring the problem wouldn't solve the situation or eliminate the odor. Whatever caused the stench had to be removed.

You know those thoughts that lurk in your head ... the ones that remind you about the person who wronged you? The person who said those horrible things, or took what should have been yours, or robbed your innocence?

Does that person deserve forgiveness? Probably not. Some people have done terrible things. Yet, do any of us deserve forgiveness?

An unforgiving spirit fouls up everything—including our attitude, our relationship with others and with God.

The road to Heaven is narrow. Unforgiveness gets heavy, smells, and rots from the inside out. Garbage can't enter the gates of Heaven; it won't fit and doesn't belong.

Jesus reaches out with compassion, mercy, and grace. Forgive, and you will be forgiven ~ Luke 6:37.

Heavenly Father my sin and unforgiving stinketh. I don't want anything to block Your forgiveness. Father, wash me clean in Your forgiveness as I forgive others.

~ Smith ~

Blacksmiths were an integral part of colonial America. Every facet of life was touched by this profession—from horseshoes for transportation, weapons and iron gates for protection, and tools and accessories for cooking.

According to Webster's 1828 Dictionary, a Smith is "literally, the striker, the beater; hence, one who forges with the hammer; one who works in metals; as an iron-smith; gold-smith; silver-smith."

Writers are wordsmiths. We design and forge words to give reader takeaways—providing beats of prose to strike a point. Words of truth provide fortification and protection. And words cook up new ideas and thoughts to digest and nourish. I try to craft words that carry God's light to a world engulfed in darkness, words that break open new truths and accomplish Heavenly purposes.

You too are a Smith. You've been forged by God and refined like gold. You've been gifted with the power of speech or writing to ignite a burning fire within those you meet to leave a legacy of God's love.

Heavenly Father help me to be the best at what You have called me to do. Forge in Me Your truth, so I may forge in others the truth of Your grace, mercy, and love.

~ *Leaf Me Alone!* ~

Shedding their fall coat, trees send showers of yellow and brown fluttering to the ground. The leaves blanket our backyard and the rocks of my homemade version of a tiny river. Sitting on the edge, I clear out debris to allow the water to flow free.

I want my life to resemble a clean river—sparkling with the healing, quenching of God's love, grace, and mercy. Unfortunately, daily living sometimes clogs with worry and anxiety. Leaves of life pelt never-ending problems: health concerns, career choices, economy woes, unpaid bills, parenting, relationships, etc., etc., etc. Some days the worry leaf pile looks so large, I'd need a twenty-ton blower to clear the mess.

Every day, I have to choose to trust God. If I focus on Him and His incredible power—the power that is above all powers on this earth, I don't have to worry. He is bigger than anything that can blow my way.

Maybe it's time to treat problems much like fall leaves. Rake 'em into a pile and even free fall into them a time or two. And when I get tired of messing with those dirty problems, I'm going to give them to God and let Him set them on fire.

Join me. I'll even bring the marshmallows.

Heavenly Father, thank You that I can bring my problems to You. I'm leaving (and leafing) them with You to burn them away by the light of Your love and truth!

~ *Twiddling Toothpicks* ~

Often my focus gets off track. I stare at life's difficulties instead of the amazing bounty of God-given blessings. I tried Bible verses, quotes, hymns, praise and worship songs, and yet nothing seemed to get rid of the little dark cloud. I still felt like problems were chained to my leg, and I couldn't move forward. Sniffle, whine, pout.

Then I remembered I do have a choice. (Yes, I'm rather slow at times). God's word says to resist the devil, and he will flee. I haven't been resisting, I've been a willing partner in allowing the negativity.

Instead of utilizing the Sword of the Spirit, I was twiddling toothpicks.

After rebuking my attitude and sending the enemy packing, I figuratively took my problems, placed them on God's altar, and left it for Him. Whew! Boy, I always feel so much better when I do things God's way.

This world is a tough place and often situations seem overwhelming. Please know that whatever difficulties you face; you are never alone, never without help, and never without a champion.

Heavenly Father help me to put down my proverbial toothpick of human reasoning and pick up Your powerful and almighty Sword of the Spirit!

~ Put It On The Big Screen ~

Several years ago, I had a difficult time letting go of a past hurt. To be honest, it wasn't one of my most painful moments. And the issue wasn't even so much what was done, but who did it. Someone from church, who I considered a friend, hurt my feelings.

I would take the offense to God and release it in prayer. But then the reminders would replay, and I would again wallow in self-pity and anger. I wanted everyone else to see what this person did, to put their failures on a big movie screen.

I wanted the preacher to announce in church, and to the entire world, what this person was really like.

Ah the satisfaction as everyone would be shocked at that person's failure and moved to compassion for me ... the poor, injured party.

However as I was running this scenario through my mind and taking it to its grand conclusion, I realized there was a major problem.

Would I want to be judged in the same way?

Oh my goodness – *no!* Yet, I was asking God for punishment beyond what I would ever want for myself.

If I so actively seek grace from my Savior, should I not actively give grace to others?

Forgive us our sins, as we have forgiven those who sin against us. ~ Matthew 6:12

~ *Loose Lips* ~

To warn against careless conversations that could be overheard and used by the enemy during World War II, the United States War Advertising council published posters warning — "Loose Lips Might Sink Ships."

Which led me to wonder ... as Christians do we tend to forget we are involved in daily battle?

Our struggle isn't against flesh and blood, but against the rulers, against the authorities, against the powers of this dark world and against the spiritual forces of evil in the heavenly realms ~ Ephesians 6:12.

The enemy is listening. Choose your words wisely. For by your words you will be justified, and by your words you will be condemned ~ Matthew 12:37 NASB.

What words do you want the enemy to hear? What do you want God to hear?

"Let me tell you something: Every one of these careless words is going to come back to haunt you. There will be a time of Reckoning. Words are powerful; take them seriously. Words can be your salvation. Words can also be your damnation." ~ Matthew 12:37 MSG

~ Anviled By The Past ~

Remember the old cartoons with the Coyote and Road Runner? The Coyote ordered every gadget imaginable from ACME to help him catch the Road Runner. Unfortunately either the products would fail or the coyotes own ineptitude would result in rather unappealing calamities.

Often the coyote would use an anvil in hopes of squashing the road runner. Instead, the anvil would wind up causing him harm.

Lugging around past issues without allowing for God's healing never has positive results. And when we don't forgive, we might as well strap an anvil to our backs.

As tempting as it may be to wallow in the muck of the past, there are choices. Oswald Chambers advised to "take ourselves by the scruff of the neck and shake ourselves" out of our moods. Goodness knows there are days I need a good shaking.

I can easily look at the past and grieve. I can wallow in pain, making everyone miserable. Or I can remember in Christ there is always hope. I can whine and be bent over by the weight of the past, or I can drop the anvil and walk free in Christ. Christ came not only to free us from all sin, but to free us from the past.

Jesus came to proclaim freedom for prisoners, recovery of sight for the blind, and to release the oppressed. For the Lord is the Spirit, and where the Spirit of the Lord is, there is freedom. So if the Son makes you free, you will be free indeed ~ Luke 4:18, 2 Corinthians 3:17, John 8:36.

Jesus thank You for Your saving grace and freedom. Open my eyes and help me walk and live fully aware that I am no longer anviled by the past.

~ Have You Seen My Joy? ~

I woke up today and joy was gone. I'm not sure where I left it. I've looked all over the house and yard. I've called friends looking for my joy. I've driven the streets calling out and searching. I've shopped, eaten my favorite foods, watched shows on television, even sat with my family. But I still can't find my joy.

Have you seen my joy?

I'm miserable without it. Should I post a sign on the street corner? Should I place an ad in the newspaper? Maybe even send out a missing joy alert.

But then … in the quiet, a tiny stirring, a tiny flicker of hope brightens. On my desk, in The Book with words written before time, the truth calls. The truth of where joy is found. And my soul kneels and looks up to The One who is joy.

Restore to me the joy of my salvation, and uphold me with a willing spirit. For You have been my help, and in the shadow of Your wings I sing for joy. I will go to the altar of God, to God my exceeding joy, and I will praise you. Let those who delight in righteousness shout for joy and be glad and say evermore, great is the Lord. For You have made me glad by Your work; at the works of your hands I sing for joy. ~ Psalm 51:12, 63:7, 43:4, 35:27, 92:4.

Blessed be God—He heard me praying. He proved He's on my side; I've thrown my lot in with Him. Now I'm jumping for joy, and shouting and singing my thanks to Him ~ Psalm 28:6-7 MSG.

Your words are a joy and the delight of my heart. You make known the path of life, and in Your presence is fullness of joy at Your right hand are pleasures forevermore. We shout for joy over our salvation. For You make us glad with the joy of Your presence ~ Jeremiah 15:16, Psalm 16:11, Psalm 20:5, Psalm 21:6.

Those who look to You for help will be radiant with joy; no shadow of shame will darken their faces. Rejoice in the Lord and be glad, all you who obey him! Shout for joy, all you whose hearts are pure! ~ Psalm 34:5 NLT, Psalm 32:11 NLT.

Light is sown for the righteous, and joy for the upright in heart. Make a joyful noise to the Lord, all the earth; break forth into joyous song and sing praises! Make a joyful noise to the Lord, all the earth! And let them offer sacrifices of thanksgiving, and tell of his deeds in songs of joy! ~ Psalm 97:11, 98:4, 100:1, 107:22 ESV.

Sing for joy, O heavens, and exult, O earth; break forth, O mountains, into singing! For the Lord has comforted his people and will have compassion on his afflicted. Those who sow in tears shall reap with shouts of joy! He who goes out weeping, bearing the seed for sowing, shall come home with shouts of joy, bringing his sheaves with him. Our mouth was filled with laughter, and our tongue with shouts of joy; then they said among the nations, The Lord has done great things for them. ~ Isaiah 49:13, Psalm 126:5-6, 126:2 ESV.

Now to him who is able to keep you from stumbling and to present you blameless before the presence of his glory with great joy ~ Jude 1:23-25 ESV.

Thank You Heavenly Father, in You I find my joy for You are joy!

~ The Verdict ~

God is very clear on the matter of forgiveness. Jesus told the following story to His followers in Matthew 18:23-35

A King decided to settle his accounts. The first servant owed him millions of dollars. The servant couldn't pay so the King ordered everything the servant had to be sold – along with his wife and children. The servant fell on his face and begged his master for patience and promised he would pay back everything he owed. The King felt pity for this man and pardoned his debt.

The forgiven servant left and came across a fellow servant who owed him a few thousand dollars. The forgiven man grabbed his fellow servant by the throat and demanded instant payment. The fellow servant fell before him begging for a little more time. The forgiven man wouldn't wait; he had his debtor thrown in prison. When the king heard what happened he was furious.

The King's reply, "I canceled all your debt because you begged me to. Shouldn't you have had mercy on your fellow servant just as I had on you?" In anger the king turned him over to the jailers to be tortured until he paid back all he owed. Then Jesus reminds us that this is how our heavenly Father will treat us if we don't forgive our brothers. Ouch.

Picture a courtroom. The jury is in place, the lawyers are ready, and the judge sits on the bench. The person who wronged you is brought into the room.

You scream, jump to your feet, and hit the person over and over again. The bailiff and lawyers try to restrain you, but you can't be contained because that person does not deserve forgiveness. The judge bangs his gavel and pronounces his verdict – "as you have spoken, so it will be done to you. If that person doesn't deserve forgiveness, neither do you."

Our choices are limited. We can forgive others and be forgiven. Or, we can keep a tally of their sins. The problem is, our sins also continue to be tallied.

Which sins do you want remaining on your record?

When God tells us to forgive, He is not questioning the reality of your wounds, or the level of your pain, or that you have been sinned against. Forgiveness is not what you do for them; it is a gift to yourself. And with that gift comes, freedom, peace of mind, and right fellowship and relationship with God.

Forgiveness does not release their debt. Forgiveness of others releases our debt.

If you forgive men when they sin against you, your heavenly Father will also forgive you. But if you don't forgive men their sins, your Father will not forgive your sins ~ Matthew 6:14-15.

The person most hurt by not forgiving ... is you.

Heavenly Father I don't want anything or anyone to block Your forgiveness. I forgive.

~ *Squatters* ~

When God led the Israelites out of the wilderness, He granted each tribe a portion of land, an inheritance. Unfortunately much of the land was already occupied and many of the tribes allowed the squatters to remain. And the negative results remain evident today.

When we make Jesus Lord of our lives and become Christ followers, we are granted an eternal inheritance, a new life. However, many Christians aren't living unhindered lives. They aren't walking in freedom because they haven't evicted the squatters remaining in their minds and thoughts.

What are you allowing to continue squatting in the territory of your mind? Shame? Pride? Fear? Spirit of entitlement? Anxiety? Worry? Ungodly desires? Depression? Past heartache and pain? Unforgiveness? Complaining?

We can kick out the squatters.

We can take thoughts captive, cast our cares on the Lord, and lay aside every encumbrance. We don't have to be anxious or live in fear. We can replace negative thoughts with thoughts that are true, honorable, and right, and pure, and lovely, and admirable, and excellent and worthy of praise.

Want to live a free life in Christ? Kick out the squatters!

Heavenly Father with Your help, I'm taking those thoughts captive and living squatter free!

~ *Choosing Joy* ~

Two children were baptized in the church where we attended in Texas. During the baptism, friends and families were invited to stand in their honor. The two rows in front of us stood, including three young girls probably no older than three or four. The girls watched with great anticipation, tiny hands clasped to hold in their excitement as the preacher explained who was being baptized and their faith walk.

Much to the delight of those close enough to watch, the little girls clapped, jumped up and down, and squealed in glee as their friends were baptized. I couldn't help wondering if the angels in Heaven were doing the same.

I want to be like those little girls, living a life full of joy. I want to be like our dog who cranes to stick his head out of the car window and wags as he goes through life. I want to walk with childlike faith knowing everything will be okay because God is in control.

Though His Precious Son, Jesus, He is the One who takes a sinner and makes them whole. He takes the past and renews and restores. He gives hope for the future. In Him, we find joy for today and tomorrow.

Oh Father, help me always choose joy.

Woo hoo! Rejoicing forever in our awesome God.

Let all who take refuge in You be glad; let them ever sing for joy. Spread Your protection over them, that those who love Your name may rejoice in You. Rejoice in the Lord always. I will say it again: Rejoice! ~ Psalm 5:11, Philippians 4:4

~ Open Eared and Open Eyed ~

What if you called your Very Best Friend (VBF) every single day at 8:00 in the morning? But one day you do something different. Instead of calling, you stop by their house. But your VBF doesn't answer the door.

So you send an e-mail to check and see if they are okay. But your VBF won't answer.

So you send them flowers. But the flower delivery person says your VBF wouldn't even come to the door. So you leave a huge sign on their front yard telling your VBF how much you love them. But they never come out to look. So you mail your VBF a letter. But the letter comes back return to sender.

So you ask another friend to tell your VBF hello. But that friend says your VBF friend won't believe you want to talk to them unless you call them exactly at 8:00 in the morning.

So the next day, you call your VBF. And your VBF tells you they didn't think you cared because you didn't call, and if you really were their VBF you would call every day exactly at 8:00 in the morning.

The scenario is a little over the top, however do we do the same thing with God? Do we think God will only communicate to us in one way?

Think of all the ways God speaks to us – through His Word, through a preacher or Bible teacher, through moments of praise, through enjoying the beauty of His creation, through Godly insight from others, through Bible studies, or through video or audios that bring us closer to His presence.

God is speaking.

Will we be open to hear and see the unique ways He communicates?

Heavenly Father, You are my VBF. Keep me open eared and open eyed to respond to You. Tender my heart to always be aware of You and the call of Your unfailing love.

~ *What Are You Listening To?* ~

What are you listening to?
The voices in your head?
The voices from your past?
The voices around you?

Or will you listen to …
The Voice that knows you inside and out.
The Voice that will show you the way.
The Voice that speaks eternal truth.
The Voice that loves you with an unfailing love.

The very voice of God.

My sheep hear My voice, and I know them, and they follow Me.
Look! I stand at the door and knock. If you hear my voice and open the door,
I will come in, and we will share a meal together as friends.
~ John 10:27 NASB, Revelation 3:20 NLT

~ Breaking Free From The Cocoon ~

My body is altering, and I'm not very fond of some of these physical changes. I've been asking God to help me to see through the proper perspective—His eternal perspective. As I watch the body age, the flesh becoming looser, and the hair turning gray, I remember I am made for another world.

Bodies are only temporary, souls are eternal. Every day as the aging process continues, we get closer to our final destination. Our souls provisionally cocooned in an earthly body. The cocoon withers and shrivels in anticipation of what is to come. And one day soon our souls will burst free, our wings will unfurl, and we'll fly straight to our eternal home.

Heavenly Father, help me to embrace the aging process with joy. Because soon I'll leave behind the failing flesh and fly straight to You!

While we live in these earthly bodies, we groan and sigh, but it's not that we want to die and get rid of these bodies that clothe us. Rather, we want to put on our new bodies so that these dying bodies will be swallowed up by life. ...Anyone who belongs to Christ has become a new person. The old life is gone; a new life has begun! ~ 2 Corinthians 5:4, 17 NLT

~ Secret Agents ~

When I was a little girl, I loved pretending to be a secret agent. With imagination ripe for adventure, the glider on my friend's swing set became the transportation to clandestine missions.

Rescues would be made, secrets recovered, and prisoners released. My friend and I would dangle precariously over imaginary lava, shark, or lion pits, then slide to safety. Just thinking about those days makes me smile.

I still feel like a secret agent, because Christians are here on a mission working undercover in a world held hostage. We live, walk, and move through enemy territory, telling others the Good news about our Jesus who sets captives free.

I'm sending you off to open the eyes of the outsiders so they can see the difference between dark and light, and choose light, see the difference between Satan and God, and choose God. I'm sending you off to present my offer of sins forgiven, and a place in the family, inviting them into the company of those who begin real living by believing in me. ~ Acts 26:16-18 MSG.

Heavenly Father, I'm reporting for assignment. Use me today and every day to fulfill the mission for which I've been created. I have Your book to guide me, Your Spirit to lead me, and the armor of God to protect me. Keep my eyes on You and my ears always ready for Your call.

~ Why Didn't You Tell Me? ~

I had a disturbing image as I was thinking about the lost.

What if...

as we walked into Heaven those we didn't tell about Christ were lined up and asked ...

Why didn't you tell *me*?

This is how much God loved the world: He gave his Son, his one and only Son. And this is why: so that no one need be destroyed; by believing in him, anyone can have a whole and lasting life. God didn't go to all the trouble of sending his Son merely to point an accusing finger, telling the world how bad it was. He came to help, to put the world right again. Anyone who trusts in him is acquitted; anyone who refuses to trust him has long since been under the death sentence without knowing it. And why? Because of that person's failure to believe in the one-of-a-kind Son of God when introduced to him.
~ John 3:16-18 MSG

Go into all the world and preach the gospel to every creature. He who believes and is baptized will be saved; but he who does not believe will be condemned.
~ Mark 15:15-16 NKJV

~ *Invitation Of Adversity* ~

Have you ever tried to rescue a wounded animal? No matter how good your intentions, you are in for a battle.

How often do we fight God?

God gently places us on a bed of adversity and we gnash our teeth, bite, howl, growl, and attack. We question God's goodness, stumble and wail on the things we don't understand. We don't want to face trials.

We want to be so protected that our spines have the consistency of Jello. Our eyes remain so fixed on the ways of the world; we don't see God's ways. We overlook the fact we exist for eternity. We forget God's way is best, His plans are always for good, and His love is unfailing.

God's invitation of adversity is a calling to step beyond the ordinary to go deeper, to see God's hand move in ways we didn't think possible. The storms of adversity blow away the soul's chaff and forces our roots deeper. Adversity raises the dead, opens the eyes of the blind, spreads the gospel, and raises up warriors.

St. Augustine wrote, "In my deepest wound, I saw Your glory and it dazzled me."

God's glory is displayed in the back-against-the-Red-Sea moments, in the lion's den, the fiery furnaces, and in the battle scars of life. Afflictions, adversities, trials, troubles, and suffering drive us to our knees and straight to God's heart. For in His loving heart we find all we need.

Dear brothers and sisters, when troubles come your way, consider it an opportunity for great joy. For you know that when your faith is tested, your endurance has a chance to grow. So let it grow, for when your endurance is fully developed, you will be perfect and complete, needing nothing. Not only that, but we rejoice in our sufferings, knowing that suffering produces endurance, and endurance produces character, and character produces hope, and hope does not put us to shame, because God's love has been poured into our hearts through the Holy Spirit who has been given to us. ~ James 1:2-5 NLT, Romans 5:3-5 ESV

~ *Intense Love* ~

Holocaust survivor, Corrie Ten Boom wrote, "Forgiveness is the key that unlocks the door of resentment and the handcuffs of hate. It is a power that breaks the chains of bitterness and the shackles of selfishness."

In 1947 Corrie traveled to Munich preaching about God's forgiveness. Most of her talks were met by silence. People listened silently and they left silently. This time was different. A heavy-set man in a gray overcoat, carrying a brown felt hat, moved toward her. And she knew as she studied his face, he had been one of the guards at the concentration camp where she and her sister had been, the very place her sister had died.

The man extended his hand as he stood in front of her, complimenting her on the message. It was the first time since her release she had been face-to-face with one of her captors and her blood seemed to freeze in her veins. He did not remember her, but she remembered him. She fumbled in her pocketbook rather than take his hand.

He told Corrie he had become a Christian. He knew God forgave him for all the cruel things he did in the past, yet he also asked for her forgiveness. His hand remained outstretched, and Corrie stood rigid.

She knew deep down she had to forgive, that God requires us to forgive in order to receive forgiveness. She had seen the proof in her own life and the lives of those in the home she had established for those abused by the Nazis. The victims who forgave their enemies were able to heal and return to their lives. The ones who did not forgive, who remained in bitterness, remained invalids.

Corrie realized forgiveness is something we do regardless of how we feel. It's not an emotion. She prayed silently asking Jesus to help her and woodenly she thrust her hand in his.

At their contact, she felt a current run down her shoulder and into their joined hands. At that moment she said she had never felt God's love as intensely as she did then.

Heavenly Father thank You for the intense love that flows freely from You when we forgive others. You are a just and righteous God. Thank You that You promise that vengeance is Yours and we can trust You to do what is right. And when we release our hurts and wounds to You, Your healing and freedom comes to us.

~ *What Fills You?* ~

What fills your time, your thoughts, your days, and your nights? Are you filling yourself with the world's perspective or God's eternal perspective? Are you filling yourself with things that honor God? Are you filling yourself with His word and His truth?

Do we run on empty so often because we forget to fill ourselves with The One true source of all peace, joy, truth, hope, faithfulness, strength, mercy, grace, and love? Fill up, dear friends. Read the verses below and fill up!

I will be filled with joy because of you. I will sing praises to your name, O Most High. ~ Psalm 9:2 NLT.

The LORD is my strength and shield. I trust him with all my heart. He helps me, and my heart is filled with joy. I burst out in songs of thanksgiving. ~ Psalm 28:7 NLT.

May all who search for you be filled with joy and gladness in You. May those who love your salvation repeatedly shout, The LORD is great! ~ Psalm 40:16 NLT.

Happy are the people you choose and invite to stay in your court. We are filled with good things in your house, your holy Temple. ~ Psalm 65:4 NCV.

The whole earth is filled with awe at your wonders; where morning dawns, where evening fades, You call forth songs of joy. ~ Psalm 65:8 NIV.

But let the godly rejoice. Let them be glad in God's presence. Let them be filled with joy. ~ Psalm 68:3 NLT.

May all who search for you be filled with joy and gladness in You. ~ Psalm 70:4 NLT.

I have told you these things so that you will be filled with my joy. Yes, your joy will overflow!" ~ John 15:11 NLT.

Heavenly Father, thank You for Your joy. Thank You that as we stay in Your presence, praise You, and read Your word, we can be filled with joy.

~ Why Didn't Anyone Believe? ~

Why did those who Jesus touched, fed, and healed, demand He be executed? Why did those who knew Jesus best not believe He would rise again? Why wasn't anyone waiting in anticipation for His return? Was everyone so convinced Jesus came only to bring an earthly kingdom they couldn't understand His death was only the beginning?

Why didn't anyone believe?

And then I wonder, how many times do our own thoughts and ideas keep us from believing God's amazing plans?

Heavenly Father, put to death anything in me that stands in Your way. Help me remove my thoughts and ideas to be open to Yours. I want to be waiting in anticipation, believing and open to all You have planned. Take all of me, to be raised in new life with You.

No eye has seen, no ear has heard, and no mind has imagined what God has prepared for those who love Him. ~ 1 Corinthians 2:9 NLT

~ *Burn Them* ~

In the Old Testament the Israelites had to offer sacrifices for their sins. And that sacrifice gave them the visual of the flames consuming the things that stood in the way of a relationship with a righteous God.

The smell, the smoke rising to Heaven, and the knowledge of that release, although painful to watch, had to be very freeing.

If there are things that you have had trouble releasing – things you have done or things others have done to you. If you would be willing, I want you to write those things down. Not to relive the pain, but to write them to God.

Write out everything, pray, release those issues, the people who hurt you, and give them to God. And then if you have a safe place to burn those pages. Burn them. Watch the fire consume the papers and smell and watch the smoke as it rises to Heaven.

And then when the enemy taunts with past mistakes or tries to have you walk back into the pain of your past, you'll be able to visually remember that those items have been given to God and everything falls under his justice, righteousness, and grace.

Heavenly Father I'm bringing You all those things that cause me to stumble or struggle. I don't want anything in my life that blocks me from living free in You.

~ Don't Feed The Monster ~

What if on your front porch someone left a deadly, poisonous, ravenous, wicked, rabid, crazed, flesh-eating monster? Now mind you, the monster does tend to sweet talk and try to convince you that you should just take it in and everything will work out just fine.

Unfortunately, we've all invited in the monster. We've all been hypnotized and mesmerized by his subtle soothing voice.

A lie is a monster.

Lies often slither in without us even being aware of its presence. Remember that lie someone said when you were a kid that you weren't smart? Or the lie that said you've been used and abused and no one will want you now? Or the lie that tells you that people and God wouldn't love you if they knew the truth about you? Or you're too old? Or you're too fat, too thin, too lazy, too dumb, too late, too early, too ….

Lies come in all shapes and sizes. They hook their slimy claws into minds and quietly wait to pounce when least expected. Lies cause us to believe things that aren't true about ourselves, our situation, and about others. Lies get us to behave in ways we shouldn't. Lies keep us from healing. Lies keep us miserable. Lies keep us from relationships with people. Lies keep us from a relationship with God.

So I've been wondering … what started the lie? What lies do you believe about yourself, others, or your situation? You don't have to feed the monster.

Kick out the lie monster, squash, starve, and annihilate the lies with God's truth! And The Truth will set you free.

Heavenly Father help me to know Your truth so that I won't fall for the lies of the enemy. Thank You that Your truth sets me free!

~ In His Presence ~

A conversation I had with my friend Marlyn as she was dying from cancer always sticks with me. We agreed there are places no one can go with us – except Jesus. And in His presence we find His peace.

When we dwell in God's presence we are inviting Him into our lives. We are keeping our soul open and our spiritual ears tuned to hear His voice.

Psalm 46:10 reminds us to be still and know that He is God. Even when we are moving forward at full speed we can quiet our soul. Jesus tells us to remain in Him, abiding in His presence, living in His love, John 15:4, 6-7, 9-10.

Remaining in God's presence gives us the interaction, guidance, the ability to bear fruit, and the connection to know we are loved and in His love.

The times I start worrying about something or my soul becomes disquieted and anxious, I know I have stepped away from God's presence. When I chose to turn to Him, quiet my soul with His words, immerse myself in a praise song, I can feel that calming as I move back into His presence. When we live in obedience, we live in love.

Dwelling and remaining in His presence is making God our destination and our ultimate desire, it's a road trip to peace. When we first moved to Idaho we were living in an apartment while waiting for our Texas house to sell.

Our weekends were spent exploring. We'd chart a course and head out. Since I would make my poor, sweet husband pull over every fifteen minutes to take photos, our short trips would take all day.

We wanted to see more of Idaho, and each time we set out we had a destination and goal. And even more so, we were out to enjoy the ride.

I want to be like that with God. Believing, trusting, and having faith in His guidance, staying in obedience with His direction, because He knows the best way to get us safely home. We can always trust God's guidance and believe Him to lead us.

Heavenly Father thank You that You establish our steps and delight in our way. Thank You that You hold our hands and keep us safe.

~ *Tubular Vision* ~

Without contacts or glasses, my eyesight is one step above legally blind. I have to pay extra so my lenses don't look like coke bottles. Without vision correction, I can't see the alarm clock next to the bed without getting within inches.

My spiritual eyes at times aren't any better. I say I believe God, and yet when something comes up, I tailspin into worry or take matters into my own hands—as though I could actually find my way out of a paper bag. I have absolutely no clue what tomorrow holds. I think I do. I make my plans, but only God really knows the way. I try to see things from the right perspective.

However if I don't filter life through the reality of God and His Word, I might as well be looking through binoculars made of toilet paper tubes!

Heavenly Father, help me to remember to look to You and Your word before I take even one step so I may see my way clearly through life, and see life clearly through You.

~ *Father, May I?* ~

Did you ever play the game, "Mother May I", or what some call "Captain May I"? One person would be the "Mother" or the "Captain." That person would stand facing away from the other players – "children" or crewmembers."

The players take turns asking "Mother/Captain, may I ___?" and makes a movement suggestion. For example, Johnny might ask, "Mother/Captain, may I take five steps forward?" The leader either replies "Yes, you may" or "No, you may not do that, but you may ___ instead" and inserts his/her own suggestion. Such as "Johnny you may take giant/regular/baby steps/scissor steps/bunny hops/frog leaps/ballet steps, forward or backward."

The players usually move closer but are sometimes led farther away. Even if the leader makes an unfavorable suggestion, the player must still perform the action. The first player to reach the location of the leader wins the game.

What if the lead person is your best friend? Your very best-friend-forever (BFF). Wouldn't the game be fun? No matter what you ask, or what movement you make, you know your BFF will make sure you come out ahead. You can't lose. Even if they tell you to sit and wait. The wait would be worth it, because your friend will make sure you win.

What if we didn't make a move until we checked with our Heavenly Father? What if we enjoy the journey, waiting in anticipation for His answer? Delighting in whatever He decides. Moving in whatever way He says to move. Knowing whatever happens, in the end we always win.

The steps of a man are established by the Lord, and He delights in his way. When he falls, he shall not be hurled headlong, because the Lord is the One who holds his hand. The Lord will always lead you. He will satisfy your needs in dry lands and give strength to your bones. You will be like a garden that has much water, like a spring that never runs dry. ~ Psalm 37:23-24 NAS, Isaiah 58:11 NCV

~ *Grab The Leash!* ~

Our little dog, Chipper, can't wait to get out and explore the world. He doesn't care where he's going—he just wants to get there as fast as possible. We try to keep him close, but no, he thinks he knows so much better. Pull … cough … tug … hack … never stop. He pulls, and the pressure continues on the collar because he is too busy sniffing, pawing, and exploring his world.

Chipper has a love/hate relationship with his leash. He loves the walk, but would prefer to run free. He doesn't realize his leash is not for punishment, but for safety. He doesn't know which path to take, thinks every dog will be his friend, not realizing he is but an appetizer for a big dog. He could have a great walk without pressure if he would just stay close.

I'm as guilty as the dog. I've complained about the unbearable pressure of life's pace, begging God to give me extra slack so I could go play on a different path.

"Come on God … pull, hack, let's go … cough." Or thinking I know the best plans, I've plowed ahead, and then wondered why on earth there were so many struggles, problems, and difficulties.

An intimate relationship with God gives us direction in our daily walk without angst or worry. God knows the safest paths. Fluidity in our lives comes by knowing God's word and His character. Constant guidance comes from consistent contact.

The path won't always be easy, and often our walk will lead us weary and panting. But God always knows the best way. Our pathway isn't just about us. Our pathway to eternal life leaves footprints through the mundane daily chores, activities, and life difficulties that lead others to Heaven's door.

God is a loving Father who knows the best way to bring us safely home. Trust Him, relax, and enjoy the journey. You couldn't be in better Hands.

Heavenly Father, thank You for Your guidance. Forgive me when I pull on the leash. I'm so grateful You always know the way.

~ Soul GPS ~

I am directionally challenged. No matter which way I am facing, the direction seems to be north. Without the automobile's handy dandy built-in compass, I would be wandering aimlessly for years. If someone gives directions using north, south, east, and west, they might as well be talking in a foreign language. I need landmarks and turns with rights and lefts. Many an unplanned road-trip has been made, which would be reclassified as explorations. I'm never lost, just exploring.

Fortunately God never loses me, but I would love a soul GPS. I'd never get lost, sidetracked, or out of His perfect will. The wonderful thing is God gives us His word to direct and light our way. He says call and He will tell us amazing things we didn't know. God promises to make us wise, show us where to go, and guide us down delightful paths.

Sounds like a great reason to always keep our soul GPS plugged into God's Holy Spirit. Anyone up for a God-given road trip?

Heavenly Father, I'm staying plugged into Your Holy Spirit. Guide me along Your perfect paths. I'm ready to roll!

~ Psalm 119:105, Jeremiah 33:3, Psalm 32:8, Proverbs 3:17

~ *Out Of The Box* ~

I'm out of the box. God gently nudged me off the beaten path. I'm thrilled, excited, curious, and a little scared. Not fearful of being left on my own, but afraid of messing up. It's hard finding the way when you can't follow the well-worn trails others have blazed.

Part of me wants to run back and forth trying every door possible until I find the "right" one, another part wants to sit still in quiet confidence, and still another wants to just curl up in a ball on the floor and sob. *Heavenly Father, I stepped forward. What do I do now?*

God has us all on unique journeys, and many times God tells us to go when we don't even know where we're going. Some of us have traveling companions, others go alone. The Bible tells us a man's mind plans his way, but the Lord directs his steps *and* makes them sure. And when people's steps follow the Lord, God is pleased with their ways. Because He knows the plans He has for us, plans to prosper us and not to harm us, plans to give us hope and a future.

So even when the pathway is unclear, even when we're out of our comfortable boxes, we can be assured He will lead and guide us on His appointed way.

Heavenly Father, guide my steps as You promised; don't let any sin, my own wayward thoughts, or my own ideas, control me. I will press on toward the goal to win the prize for which You have called me heavenward in Christ Jesus. I'm following, trusting with all my heart, not leaning on my own understanding, and acknowledging You in all my ways. Please lead me on Your straight path.

~ Genesis 12:1, Jeremiah 29:11, Proverbs 16:9, Psalm 37:23, Psalm 119:133, Philippians 3:14.

~ Unique ~

How often do we miss what God is doing, because we are so busy watching for how we think He should work, lead, and heal?

When God led people, no two journeys were the same. When Jesus healed people, He didn't heal the same way twice. Some were hands-on healings, others were from a distance.

When God routed the enemies of the Israelites, He used some pretty creative methods. Think of the plagues against Egypt, they weren't just done for random effect, they were against the "gods" of the Egyptians. Joshua and the city of Jericho is a great example. God told Joshua and all the people to march around Jericho for six days. Not to fight. Not to taunt. Not to show off their mighty army. On the seventh day, all they had to do was blow the trumpet and shout. God collapsed the walls and Jericho was defeated. Not exactly the strategic war plan you'll see used by most generals. God's ways are definitely more than we can imagine or conceive.

God created each of us in unique ways, for unique callings, for unique paths. No two of us are alike. And how God will work in your life and in mine will be unique. Let's remember to keep our eyes and ears open to hear and watch the unique ways God works.

Heavenly Father thank You for making each one of us unique. Help me to always remember that nothing is impossible for You, and in knowing that I can rest assured You have some amazing, incredible unique ways You will work in my life.

~ *The Color Of Trials* ~

During a marathon ultrasound session and mammograms, the doctor found several problem areas. Since I was bleeding from an area that should not be bleeding, my seventh surgery was scheduled.

Do I believe God heals? Yes! Do I have faith God will heal me? You betcha! I have no doubt God will take great care of me, just don't know what will be required during some of the journey. Thankfully the surgery went well and although tissue was removed, no further treatment was necessary.

During the writing of this devotion, I changed the color cartridge in my printer. Even though the page on the computer was full of colors, the printed pages were ugly, mottled, and yellow.

A quick removal of the offending cartridge and the replacement with a new one, fixed the problem. The colors were again vibrant.

When we allow God to work in our lives there is renewal. I have scars from my head to my toes that tell of my life journey. Some are funny stories, some are not, but they all changed me. My life ink at times was mottled and yellow.

Here on earth we can't see the heavenly brush-strokes God is painting in our lives through hardships, trials, and difficulties. When we allow Him to come in and show us His perspective, our life pages change to His vibrant colors.

We don't know what tomorrow will hold, but we can be assured God will never allow anything in our lives that is not for a higher good and colored in His love.

And we know that all things work together for good to those who love God, to those who are the called according to His purpose. ~ Romans 8:28 NKJV

~ *Partial Or Full Surrender* ~

Rummaging through boxes I've found all sorts of fun items—sweet, memories galore. A copy of an e-mail I had sent to my sister-in-law described the following scene. Our son, Scott was four at the time.

Scott and Dennis were wrestling. Full contact, you know. Dennis had Scott pinned for a quick three count. Scott, flat on his back and always fun and creative, raised his legs saying he still wasn't pinned. When that wouldn't hold water, he commented he wasn't fully down since his fingers and toes were up.

Makes me wonder how often I tell God I'm surrendering to His perfect will but still have my proverbial fingers and toes sticking in the air.

When God asks us to surrender, He's not seeking to make us less of who we are, but more of who we are truly meant to be. Interesting isn't it? Living a joyful life as a Christian involves surrender.

We choose to believe, choose to focus, choose to take every thought captive, choose to surrender. Choose to cast our cares on Jesus and not worry. Choose to accept his joy and peace. Choose to obey. Choose to walk in His ways. Our choices show who we serve. And choosing full surrender to God, gives us full freedom for Him to work in our lives.

Choose today who you will serve. ~ Joshua 24:15

~ Do You Believe? ~

Years ago, a situation arose at the company where my husband worked. Positions were being jostled and people removed. We could see no earthly way this would work in our favor. We agonized and prayed, but resigned ourselves to future changes and issues. Would the house need to be prepared for another move, what would we do, where would we go? How on earth could God fix this one and what could we do to help? What could "I" do to fix it?

Oh, the tossing, turning, and nervous agony as I mulled over the desperate measures I believed would be needed. Then a quiet voice in my soul whispered, "Do you believe *He can* do it?" Without hesitation I agreed I believed God would handle this situation in several different ways.

"No", the nudging came again, "Do you believe *He will* do it?" I thought, well of course I believe. I believed God would work things out based on my understanding – a, b, c would happen, or option x, y, z, or a combination of the two.

Then the question came, "Do you believe *I* can do it?"

Ouch.

The same God who calmed the raging storm, parted the red sea, and conquered the grave, the same God who says He loves me with an everlasting love, and who has my name inscribed on the palms of His hands -- asks if I will believe. Belief, total and absolute belief that He can and would fix the situation, with His methods, His timing, and His perfect will.

The reality that the eternal God is in control finally seeped into my thick brain. Yes, He can do it!

Within the year God had rectified the insurmountable problem, without any of the drastic measures I would have deemed entirely necessary.

The solution was found not by earthly hands or by earthly means, but by the God of heaven who is the God of the impossible.

A few years later, my husband's job was outsourced. Only God knew the long, long, long wait of 448 days without a job and then waiting ten more months for our Texas house to sale. And only God knew the wonderful outcome.

A calming in our souls takes place when we grasp the concept of God's faithfulness, power, and love. Remember, The One who saved you will never fail you.

Thank You Father that nothing is too hard for you. I believe You can do all things!

~ Faith Walking ~

Enoch walked with God ~ Genesis 5:24. I've always been fascinated with Enoch. There is so little known about him. The thing I found interesting is the Bible doesn't tell us Enoch held major revivals, or wrote hundreds of books about God, or that he was a major speaker, but only that he chose to walk with God.

No qualification on Enoch's achievements but on his relationship. Wow. Walking with God is a relationship between creator and His child. Walking is believing moment by moment that God is who He says He is, and that God will meet us at our every point of need.

Isn't it an incredible thought that choosing to walk with God, loving and serving Him would be the ultimate achievement? And what's awesome about that is any one of us can do the same. No matter who we are, where we live, our health issues, our financial status ... we can walk with God.

Heavenly Father, I want to walk in faith every day with You.

~ Walking In Belief ~

In the 1800's George Müller was a thief, liar, and gambler—until God touched his heart. A changed man, Müller began preaching, and then felt the call to help poor children.

He recorded in his personal journal how he desired to show God's faithful provision. "It is true that the faith which I am able to exercise is God's own gift. He alone supports it, and He alone can increase it. Moment by moment, I depend on Him." Every page reveals God's daily, consistent, provision for each need—clothing, food, and shelter. Not once, did Müller tell anyone the needs for himself or his ministry—except God. And God met each and every need in awesome and abundant ways. Many times grace was said over empty plates, only to have food delivered before the prayer was finished.

Believing completely in Philippians 4:19 that God will meet every need. Year after year, day after day, moment by moment, George Müller took every need to his Heavenly Father.

And in George Müller's lifetime, he established 117 schools which educated over 120,000 children and through his orphanages he cared for 18,000 orphans. Eighty-two missionaries were supported, 4,000 Bibles were distributed, and over 1 million tracts and portions of scriptures.

George Müller lived and walked his faith. Oh that we would do the same!

Heavenly Father, help me to walk believing and trusting in You!

~ All We Need For Every Need ~

God is our provider – for all our needs. Not just one or two things, not just the "big" ones. But for everything. We might think we need a new car, new house, and the latest fashions. Or perhaps an awesome chocolate bar that doesn't have any calories. But God knows best and God will provide for every need.

Regardless of circumstances, situations, or requirements, God will provide everything necessary. And with those truths, comes an amazing freedom.

When sleep has been limited, I can be assured God knows exactly the amount of rest my body needs to get through the day. When the days seem too short or too long, I know God is timeless. When the checkbook funds are small, God's provision is sufficient. When the body is weak, God's power is unending and inexhaustible. When guidance is needed, God's wisdom is always available. There is no problem too big or too difficult for God.

I'm breaking out in a new song... There ain't no sickness rough enough, ain't no trauma tough enough, ain't no problem big enough, to keep God's love from me and you!

So my friends, rest easy in God's grace and peace, (or sing with me!) for God is truly all we need for every need.

Grace and peace be multiplied to you in the knowledge of God and of Jesus our Lord; seeing that His divine power has granted to us everything pertaining to life and godliness, through the true knowledge of Him who called us by His own glory and excellence. ~ 2 Peter 1:2-3 NASB

~ *Demolishing Strongholds* ~

For several weeks, our Saturday morning prayer group "camped out" in 2 Corinthians 10:3-6, "For though we walk in the flesh, we do not war according to the flesh, for the weapons of our warfare are not of the flesh, but divinely powerful for the destruction of fortresses. We are destroying speculations and every lofty thing raised up against the knowledge of God, and we are taking every thought captive to the obedience of Christ, and we are ready to punish all disobedience, whenever your obedience is complete."

God's word is active and alive, constantly revealing new truths. And the deeper we go, digging for treasure, in God's word, the more we learn, grow and water our faith. And the more time we spend with God, the brighter His truth shines.

Prayer isn't using a secret code or combination, it's coming before God's throne to listen, to praise Him, and wait on the guidance of the Holy Spirit. We are learning to take what is troubling us in prayer, to take every thought captive, to find God's solution and truth.

Through prayer and the power of God's word, we can bomb the enemy. And with God's spiritual weapons and divine power we demolish fortresses and strongholds. There is no sin too difficult for God's conquering power.

Woo hoo, anyone up for some major demolition?

Thank You Heavenly Father that my sins were demolished in the grace of Your Son, Jesus Christ. Help me to demolish any strongholds in my life that limit my freedom in You.

~ Ice, Painters, And Angels ~

Gray-green, clouds billowed on the evening horizon. With a quick goodbye to my co-workers, I hurried to my car. Rain fell and quickly morphed into sleet. The windshield wipers flapped at full speed, and I gripped the wheel as I drove the winding back roads to my parent's home in the country.

Slowing down for a curve, my tires lost traction. The car spun out of control, skidded sideways and crashed into a deep ditch. Rattled but unscathed, I sat praying, wondering what to do. My car was stuck.

Thirty minutes from home and without a cell phone, my options were to walk or sit and wait. If I waited, my parents wouldn't know I was missing until later that night, and they wouldn't know which country road I had taken.

Several farm houses sat off the road, but even to reach them would be a long walk. The only person within walking distance was a young man who had his checking account at the bank where I worked. I didn't know him well. I was a teenage bank teller, and he was a flirt. Thinking perhaps he might be my best opportunity, I made my way up the ditch.

A beat-up, old station wagon stopped next to me and the passenger window rolled down. "Can I drive you somewhere?" The driver, an elderly man wearing stained painters coveralls, waited for my answer.

The freezing rain picked up in intensity. I hesitated and glanced at the abundance of paint brushes, rollers, and paint cans spread throughout his vehicle. Cold and with limited choices, I opened the door and sat in his car. "I know someone nearby. He lives in a trailer up the road. Could you take me there?"

He looked at me, his gaze unwavering. "How well do you know him?" Somehow, I could see my dad asking the same question.

I squirmed at his fatherly scrutiny. "Not well, he has an account at the bank where I work."

He shook his head. "I won't take you there. How far do you live?"

"About thirty minutes. But you don't have to drive me that far."

Again his gaze locked into mine. "Do you have anyone you know well, or your parents know who lives closer?"

I couldn't think of anyone for a few minutes, until I remembered a family friend. "Yes sir. One of my mom's friends lives about ten minutes away."

He nodded and we drove in silence.

The house stood nestled off the road in a stand of trees, the man pulled down the wet pine-straw covered driveway and stopped. I thanked him and offered to pay for his trouble. Declining my offer, he waited as I ran to the house.

My mom's friend greeted me with open arms. A breeze filtered through the trees. I looked back. The pine-straw was undisturbed. My rescuer was gone.

Life is full of unseen dangers. Thankfully we have a God who protects, guides, and holds our hand through the storms of life. And sometimes, He even sends someone wearing painter's coveralls to carry us safely home.

Heavenly Father thank You that even when life is cold and scary, we are never out of Your loving care.

~ *Down In My Heart Joy* ~

Weepy and weary, my proverbial tail dragged behind me. No real cause. Just felt sad. I knew I was following God, knew I had done the right things, even knew I was accomplishing what God had called me to accomplish. I felt lonely, and not even that I had a reason to be lonely. It's just hard sometimes following God off the beaten path.

I was standing in the kitchen when I became aware of a song playing in my head. At first the song was faint, and then grew. Imagine my surprise when I realized the song was "I've got that joy, joy, joy, joy down in my heart..."

Even though at the moment I didn't "feel" joyful, I realized God's truth. As a Christian, Jesus lives in my heart. In His presence is fullness of joy. The Holy Spirit is joy. So ... I really do have joy in my heart.

Regardless how we feel, if we are Christians, we have God's joy within us.

We are the ones to choose how far down that joy resides.

Heavenly Father, I choose Your inexhaustible, always present joy! Help me to release Your joy that flows straight from Your heart to mine.

~ Climbing Out Of The Muck ~

I've yet to meet a person who doesn't have a painful memory from something they did, or from something someone else said or did to them. I'm so grateful for God's spiritual cleansing and healing.

However, I wonder how often we get uncomfortably comfortable in our (un)comfort zone. We become mucked in the muck of the pit of the past. Fortunately Christ offers freedom. With the ladder of His love, forgiveness, mercy, and grace, we can climb out. We can leave behind the muck.

Yet how many times do we fill a backpack with the mess of the past, strap it on our backs, slip and slide partway up the ladder, and never make it to the top? Or we climb out with our messy packs attached, and wonder why the stink of the past keeps stinking.

We are told to cast our burdens on the Lord (releasing the weight of it) and He will sustain us. He will never allow the righteous to be moved (made to slip, fall, or fail) ~ Psalm 55:22.

Jesus came to set the captives free. And when the Son sets us free we are free indeed ~ Luke 4:18, John 8:36.

With the freeing power of Christ in us, we can climb out of the muck and walk free.

Heavenly Father, help me to leave the muck in the muck pit and walk free in Your amazing love!

~ Does It Matter? ~

I'm a blogger, writer, speaker, and radio host. My words are on pages, blogs, and carried in the air. And I wonder if they matter. I wonder if the days I hold my heart out to the wind, if it will be ripped to shreds. I wonder if my love for God will make a difference for someone else—for the lost sheep who are wandering cold and alone, or for those who are in God's fold, yet feel so isolated.

Can we love them through a God who loves endlessly? Can what we offer be used? Can our little flames be seen through God's lens to shine on someone else?

Can who we are, be what is needed? Did a creator God, create us for fellowship with Him and fellowship for others?

Yes!

We are God's masterpiece, recreated in Jesus to do the good works God planned for us. So let your lights shine so that God will be glorified. ~ Ephesians 2:10 Matthew 5:16

Remember always, who you are, and what you do, makes a difference!

Heavenly Father thank You for creating me to be used by You to make a difference for now and for eternity!

~ The New Normal ~

Japan was rocked with earthquakes, a devastating tsunami, aftershocks and nuclear radiation. Life will never be the same for those affected by the destruction.

Illness and health issues shake our world. Any snippets of energy, strength, and pain-free moments are relished. Much like the aftershocks of an earthquake, chronic illness too has a fallout.

I have friends who have been termed chronic, inoperable, and even given a time-frame for their demise. Everyone around them is affected. The clock ticks and every ache and pain causes worry and concern. Has the cancer returned? Has the blood disease progressed? How much time do I have?

Everything changes. Nothing is the same. What happened to normal?

I've decided life is about accepting the new normal. Not looking back at what might have been, or what was lost, but looking forward. We are reminded in God's word to accept our lot in life. It's a gift from God. Because people who do this rarely look with sorrow on the past, for God has given them reasons for joy.

God is a God of new creations and fresh hope. I can contemplate who we were, the energy and strength we had, or remember that God promises to give strength to the weary and increase the power of the weak. He chooses the weak things of the world to shame the strong. We can look forward knowing that weeping may remain for a night, but rejoicing comes in the morning. We can rest knowing in the new normal God forever grants His strength and joy.

Heavenly Father, help me to look to You. Not look back at what was lost, but keep my eyes focused on You – the giver of Joy.

~ Ecclesiastes 5:19-20 Isaiah 40:29, 1 Corinthians 1:27, Psalm 30:5.

~ The Soft Knock ~

The soft knock on the door of your heart beckons, and God waits.
He will knock, but you must open.
Will you refuse and lock the door?
Will you turn away?
Will you stare longingly but never move?
Will you open, yet never allow Him to enter past the threshold?
Will you throw wide the door, enter in His presence, experience His
freedom and grace, and dine with His limitless love?
The choice is yours.

*Look! I stand at the door and knock. If you hear my voice and open the door, I
will come in, and we will share a meal together as friends. Those who are
victorious will sit with me on my throne, just as I was victorious and sat with
my Father on his throne. ~ Revelation 3:20-21 NLT*

~ The Divine Dance ~

As a writer, I've had blissful moments when the words flow free. No blocks. No disapproving self-editor who yells, "Stop. Rework it–it's not good enough." Nothing but blissful creativity.

Those moments are rare. A writer's life is hard work. There always seems to be a better way to structure a sentence. Or maybe an idea requires deeper development. Or a desperate search for a metaphor, analogy, or simile to brighten the page. Perhaps a snippet of dialogue to draw in the reader. Something always nags to do better.

But occasionally there is that experience when all is right, and the words fit perfectly together. The storyline flows and waltzes beautifully across the page—a genuine Fred Astaire and Ginger Rogers moment.

As a person with two left feet, and a writer who normally struggles with each word, those moments are a beautiful blessing.

However when I come in God's presence, I clasp my hands in His. To keep from tripping, I plant my feet on His, allowing Him to lead. Moving in tune with God, He leads me in a divine dance. In His loving grace, I glide along. The words will come. For now, I am going to enjoy the dance.

Regardless of your occupation or your calling, God waits with open arms to lead you in your divine dance.

Heavenly Father I'm placing my hands in Yours, please lead me in Your divine dance.

~ Stir It Up ~

Cooking is not my forte. Which was a well-known fact when we lived in Chicagoland. Neighbors panicked when they heard my husband's boss and wife were coming for dinner. I prepared my one "guest worthy" meal, and my helpful and worried friends showed up on our doorstep with side dishes and Hors d'oeuvres. (Yes, I had to check the dictionary on the spelling of that last word.)

As I write this, I have a timer set to remind me to stir the pot of beans cooking on the stove. Otherwise, we would have burnt bean brick for dinner. Fortunately, my poor husband is a man of few complaints when it comes to my lack of culinary skill.

Ah yes, my point? I'm still learning how to cook and use the bounty of cookbooks at my disposal. I guess they do more than just sit on a shelf. A task done with excellence takes time and practice. As with cooking, if you don't stir up your creation, it gets stagnant, burnt, or even solidified.

Paul writes to Timothy to fan into flame and stir up the gift he's been given. Regardless of our professions, or family situations, we are gifted and given opportunities for growth. We have to make the effort, keep stirring up the passions God has birthed in our hearts.

Stir it up through prayer. Stir it up with passionate diligence to read God's word. Fan the flame by pondering the wonderful truths of our wonderful God. Take time to recharge and refuel with quiet moments in God's presence.

Stir up your gifts! A hungry world waits.

That is why I would remind you to stir up (rekindle the embers of, fan the flame of, and keep burning) the [gracious] gift of God, [the inner fire] that is in you. ~ 2 Timothy 1:6 AMP

~ The Gain From The Loss ~

Whom have I in heaven but you? I desire you more than anything on earth. My health may fail, and my spirit may grow weak, but God remains the strength of my heart; he is mine forever. ~ Psalm 73:25-26 NLT

In the late 90's, I stayed active, moving, running, and playing. There was so much to do, so many places to go, people to see, fun things to accomplish. Then illness hit, and life stopped.

Too weak and ill to move, I was relegated to the bed or recliner. Even watching television or reading was too taxing. The things that once gave confidence–my strength and my abilities, slipped from my feeble fingers. I could do … nothing.

And yet in the stillness, in the complete stop of life, I found abundance. Through illness, I gained far more than I could imagine. Getting "me" out of the way, resulted in a closer walk and deeper faith in God. During the quiet journey, God blessed me with internal healing as I faced things long hidden in my past. New friendships were formed, and new opportunities opened for writing and speaking to share God's goodness. What I had lost was found in new God-given gains.

God became the source for strength and unending abilities. I went from self-confidence to God-confidence. And in His confidence, whether running, walking, or crawling, our God is able to do exceedingly, abundantly more than we can ask or imagine.

Heavenly Father help me not to focus on what illness has taken, but on what You have given. Help me to let go of what holds me to the earth, so I may fly free with You. Help me to hold onto nothing but You because with You all things are possible.

~ Zeroed In ~

Focusing on the door where I would be doing business, I walked across a parking lot. A few moments later, I found myself sprawled on the sidewalk. Fortunately, my nose broke the fall. Unfortunately, said appendage sustained damage and still has a slight tilt to the left.

Amazing how a fall shifts the viewpoint. Who knew there was actually a curb?

When trials come there is a zeroing in on the things we hold dear. Immediately the path warrants our attention, opposed to the surroundings. Life's difficulties readjust our focus.

Whether I live ten more days or fifty more years, I want to experience life to the fullest. God has walked me through the fires, through the raging waters, and never left my side. I may come out dripping wet, or charred and smokin', but I have found more of Him. I pray for health and better eyesight, but more than that I pray and beg for more of Him.

God is faithful. He is big enough to handle whatever you face today, and whatever comes your way tomorrow. There is no illness, no diagnosis, no heartache, and no problem too big for God. The same God who created all creation, set the planets in motion, and placed the stars in the sky, is the God who knows the numbers of hairs on your head.

No detail is too small, nothing in your life is overlooked, and nothing is impossible for God.

Heavenly Father regardless of the difficulties of life, help me to keep my focus zeroed in to You. Help me keep my eyes fixed on You and not my difficulties. I'm so grateful You can see everything, and that You are over all things and always in control.

~ He Picked You! ~

During my early years, I was not the strongest, tallest, or smartest. I could run fast, until my knee blew out in a pickup game of football with the big guys in the neighborhood.

During recess or gym, I was the last to be picked. If I didn't get on the bus quickly after school, the bus driver had to force someone to share a seat with me. Yes, I was, Forrestina Gump.

Even with a loving and supportive family, those lonely, painful years were difficult. At night I would snuggle in my bed with my stuffed animals, wishing and praying there would be someone who would choose me.

With God it doesn't matter how we look or even if we are the most talented. What matters is, you have been chosen–chosen by God for love.

He picks you!

Before you were made in your mother's womb, I chose you. Before you were born, I set you apart for a special work. You didn't chose me, I chose you. Even before he made the world, God loved you and chose you in Christ to be holy and without fault in his eyes. God decided in advance to adopt you into his own family by bringing you to himself through Jesus Christ. Therefore, walk in a manner worthy of your calling. ~ Jeremiah 1:5, John 15:16, Ephesians 1:4-6, Ephesians 4:4.

God picked You!

~ *Faith To Believe* ~

I sat on the couch under four blankets as a heating pad swaddled my head. After a three-day old ice-pick to the skull migraine, my body was freezing, and my head was about to explode. It wasn't my worse night ever, but man I was miserable.

For eleven years my health issues ranged from good to horrible. Since the wild ride began, I've begged and prayed for healing. That Friday night around 10:45 I laid in bed praying. Then God's words whispered in my soul, "Be healed, little one."

Heat from head to toe enveloped my body, and my migraine was gone. His wonderful presence was amazing. I prayed, rejoiced and praised, because I knew the healing wasn't only about a migraine. His words encompassed more.

I didn't suddenly feel like Popeye after a helping of spinach. I felt so much better, I knew He had healed me of chronic Lyme Disease. But even with that knowledge I knew the faith-walk had just begun. That night was a pick up your mat and walk moment. Not just about receiving the healing, but walking in the healing. Moment-by-moment trust even when I can't leap over buildings in a single bound.

My healing is complete, but my faith belief will continue to grow as I move forward. I don't want to plop back down when I'm afraid. I want to walk in faith and trust. Because if we don't risk believing – we don't walk believing. I'm believing, praising, and walking!

For everyone who has been born of God overcomes the world. And this is the victory that has overcome the world— our faith. Who is it that is victorious over [that conquers] the world but he who believes that Jesus is the Son of God [who adheres to, trusts in, and relies on that fact]. ~ 1 John 5:4 ESV, 1 John 5:5 AMP

~ True Strength ~

Thanks to weight training, I once was able to out-lift many men in the gym. I could bench press my body weight, lift the stack of 250 pounds on the leg machine, and even lifted 750 pounds using my calf muscles. Yes, that was in the past.

Unfortunately, illness derailed my strength and strength training. Too weak to walk, all I could do was sit or lie still while untreated Lyme Disease ravaged my body. But during that eleven year battle, I learned so many amazing truths. One of which is that we don't have to be strong. Our God is strong enough. Our God provides the strength. Our God is our strength.

Selwyn Hughes wrote, "Both doubt and faith are like muscles - the more you flex them, the stronger they become. When I made up my mind to accept the truth of God's Word by faith, muscles I never thought I had began to function. I decided by an action of my will to doubt my doubts and believe my beliefs."

Life is not just living redeemed lives, it's taking it to the next level, believing God can do exceedingly abundantly more than we can ask or imagine. It's about releasing the doubts because doubts can't save, and doubts do nothing but doubt. God wants you to let the doubts atrophy and the faith muscles strengthen.

So my friends, I pray that out of his glorious riches he may strengthen you with power through his Spirit in your inner being, so that Christ may dwell in your hearts through faith.

And I pray that you, being rooted and established in love, may have power, together with all the saints, to grasp how wide and long and high and deep is the love of Christ, and to know this love that surpasses knowledge—that you may be filled to the measure of all the fullness of God.

Now to him who is able to do immeasurably more than all we ask or imagine, according to his power that is at work within us, to him be glory in the church and in Christ Jesus throughout all generations, for ever and ever! Amen. ~ Ephesians 3:16-21 NIV.

~ Emergency Faith System ~

I'm scared. I'm a little girl sobbing at her Heavenly Daddy's feet. I'm tired, I've been rather proud of myself being brave, strong, and faith-filled. Gee, that wasn't too smart. Pride is not a good thing. And faith is much easier when there's something tangible you can touch or view. Not very faithy though is it?

It's so easy to say I have faith. So easy to attend church, read my Bible, and smile through life when the checkbook is balanced, health is good, family is fine, and all is right with the world. Unfortunately in the world we have trouble, real trouble, and sometimes really bad trouble. Jesus warned us we would. Yet we still wail and stumble when life hits with below-the-belt punches.

As I pondered the continual difficulties of life, I realize these are the times when we discover if our faith is real. We say we believe in God, but will we believe in God even when nothing is going our way? I'm thinking this is only a test. A test of the emergency faith filled system.

Will our emergency faith system click into gear when everything implodes around us? Or will we just implode?

Will we be able to say (and mean it), though the fig tree doesn't bud and there are no grapes on the vines, though the olive crop fails and the fields produce no food, though there aren't sheep in the pen and no cattle in the stalls, yet I will rejoice in the Lord, I will be joyful in God my Savior. ~ Habakkuk 3:17-18.

Though we face trials and tribulations, we can be filled with joy. Because trials produce patience, growing endurance, steadfastness, which works to perfect, develop and complete us. We must rest, trust, and wait on God, secure in knowing the Emergency Faith System is merely a vehicle to test and prove our genuine faith.

In the event of any emergency, God is always there. In the event of any need, God is sufficient. In the event of any fear, God shelters you in the shadow of His wings. With God all things are possible, and He will never, ever leave or forsake you.

Stay in God's word, keep heart focused on Him and your Emergency Faith System will remain activated!

~ John 16:33, 1 Peter 1:6-7, James 1:2-4, Luke 1:37, 1 Corinthians 10:14, Deuteronomy 31:8, Jeremiah 29:11, Psalm 32:10, 1 John 3:19, Romans 15:13, Psalm 27:14, Luke 8:24

~ *Treasure Hunt* ~

A friend recently asked why she couldn't feel God. I didn't have a good answer at that moment. I chewed on her question for days.

There are many times I can't "feel" God. Struggling through the pain of everyday life often results in a void of emotion. Or wandering in sin, the emptiness would leave me thirsty for His presence. However the desperation to find Him only drove me further into scripture and back into His arms--to search through His word to find the truth.

I flip pages of the Bible, hunt through my Bible software, desperate for His words. They soothe my soul, calm my fears, revive, restore, and envelop me in His love and presence.

His words beckon reminding me, The Lord is near to all who call on Him, to all who call on Him in truth. And I remember, whom have I in heaven but You? And earth has nothing I desire besides You. He promises, ask and it will be given to you; seek and you will find; knock and the door will be opened to you. I dig for treasure knowing, the kingdom of heaven is like treasure hidden in a field. ~ Psalm 145:18, Psalm 73:25, Matthew 7:7, Matthew 13:44.

Search through the pages of the Bible. Seek a relationship with God as you would seek treasure. Because when you find God, when you experience Jesus, you will find the greatest treasure known to man.

Heavenly Father thank You for the treasure of You and Your word. Help me to let nothing stand in the way of the treasures found in You.

~ Why God? ~

People question God, why He allowed things to happen, and why people go through so many difficulties. As a Christian, I see His hand in everything. Yet I wonder if there aren't many times we are the ones who should have been there to help.

Did God place us at certain places at certain times to be His hands and feet, to hear the cries of His children, and to make the difference?

I remember times I should have said more and done more. I cringe at the things I could have changed.

How many times did God press on hearts to help others and yet that pressing was ignored? How many are hurt/killed/raped/hungry/abused because we aren't listening? Are we so busy blaming God instead of being His hands and feet?

I think of where Jesus sends away those who did not feed, clothe, and care for others. ~ Matthew 25:31-46

What can we do to stop the evil and help those in need?

What have I missed? What am I missing? I don't want to live a life of depraved indifference. I'm asking God's forgiveness for the things that come to mind, and I'm asking Him what can I do now. How can I make a difference?

Pray for God to reveal His truths, His way. Pray to hear and obey. Pray we know what God would want us to do every moment of every day. Never ignoring His promptings. Never allowing fear or discomfort to block the path. Never stumbling over our own thoughts and ideas, but staying focused and zeroed in on His voice and His ways (even when we can't fathom His amazing vast plans).

Father, break me out of my view of the world to see Your world. I don't want to get stuck in the why's, but move forward with You.

~ Second Chances ~

Several years ago, Dallas Cowboy quarterback, Tony Romo, fumbled a field goal snap on a 19-yard attempt with 1:19 remaining on the clock. The Cowboys lost the game 21-20. Tony wept on the field and in the locker room. "I don't know that I've ever felt this low," Romo said. "I cost the Dallas Cowboys a playoff win. That is going to sit with me a long time."

I'm sorry the Cowboys didn't make the playoffs, but my heart goes out to Tony. It wasn't his fumble that cost the team their chance at the playoffs. One play is only a summation of the game and season—humans are fallible. No matter how good we think we can become, we can still fail. The season can't be changed, but there will be other opportunities. There is always next year.

How grateful I am for second chances. How grateful I am for a Savior who chose to die for me—even while I was still a sinner. He didn't wait until I fixed all my problems, or became a star at something. He took me as I was. Jesus knew even after I was saved, I would stumble through life, take some wrong paths, and occasionally slip into the mud. But when I turned back, He cleaned me up and gave me another opportunity.

So here I am so very grateful I can tell you that God loves you too. How do I know? Because He knows everything about me—every thought and action—and He still loves me.

God has helped me through some incredibly difficult situations, and every day I spend with Him I have found He is trustworthy, He is sufficient, and He is love.

God is the God of second chances.

Heavenly Father thank You that even though we were once living in sin, You gave us grace and mercy through Your Son, Jesus Christ.

~ *Looking For Answers?* ~

Need guidance? Fall in love with Jesus, He is the way.

Need wisdom? Fall in love with Jesus, If anyone asks, He grants wisdom.

Feeling alone? Fall in love with Jesus, He will never leave you or forsake you.

Divorced, widowed, single? Fall in love with Jesus, He will be your husband.

Family deserted you? Fall in love with Jesus, even if they desert you, He will be with you.

Hungry for more? Fall in love with Jesus, He is the bread of life.

Life left you parched? Fall in love with Jesus, He is living water.

Need comfort? Fall in love with Jesus, His comfort will overflow.

Feeling dead? Fall in love with Jesus, He is eternal life.

Can't find joy? Fall in love with Jesus, in His presence is fullness of joy.

Homeless? Fall in love with Jesus, you are forever home in Him.

Need a dinner partner? Fall in love with Jesus, He will dine with you.

Can't find anyone to listen? Fall in love with Jesus, when you call, He will hear.

Need peace? Fall in love with Jesus, He will give you His peace.

Feeling unloved? Fall in love with Jesus, His love is unfailing.

Worried? Fall in love with Jesus, He will take care of your every need.

Future looks dark? Fall in love with Jesus, He has good plans for you.

Unsure of your worth? Fall in love with Jesus, He loves you so much He died and rose again to give you hope, joy, peace, comfort, and eternal life.

For every question, to find every answer, fall in love with Jesus.

~ John 14:6, James 1:5, Deuteronomy 31:8, Isaiah 54:5, Psalm 27:10, John 6:48, John 7:38, 1 John 5:11, 2 Corinthians 1:3-4, Psalm 16:11, John 14:23, Revelation 3:20, Isaiah 58:9, John 14:27, Psalm 33:5, Matthew 6:31-34, Jeremiah 29:11, John 3:16

~ Pick Up Lines ~

First lines matter—just ask the nervous guy trying to get the attention of a cute girl. I uncovered these two "pick-up" lines:

"You're so sweet, you're going to put Hershey's out of business."

"Do you know why the sky is so gray? All the blue is in your eyes."

Groan.

As a writer, I try to pay attention to the beginning of each story. I want the first paragraph of a novel to entice the reader to keep reading.

As a Christian I want what I write and how I speak to be pick up lines. Lines that pick up weary souls. Words that pick up hurting hearts. Sentences that pick up those who are worried and fearful, picked up with the truth of God's protection and provision.

Let's all strive to be pick-up artists. Ready to pick one another up with God's wonderful words.

Heavenly Father, help me to be a person who picks up others by making sure the words of my mouth and the medication of my heart is always pleasing to You.

~ Dwelling And Abiding ~

I long to dwell with God, stay in the shadow of His wings; remain with Him forever, held continually safe, abiding in His love.

And the wonderful news is, God's word shows us how...

He who dwells (*remain, sit, abide, have one's abode, to stay*) in the shelter (*covering, shelter, hiding place, secret place*) of the Most High will abide (*lodge, remain, dwell*) in the shadow of the Almighty. *Jesus said,* Dwell (*to remain, abide, to sojourn, tarry, not to depart, to continue to be present, to be held, kept, continually, to continue to be, not to perish, to last, endure, live, in, to remain as one*) in Me, and I will dwell in you. Just as no branch can bear fruit of itself without abiding in the vine, neither can you bear fruit unless you abide in Me. If you keep my commandments, you will abide (*to remain, sojourn, tarry, not to depart, to continue to be present, to be held, kept, continually, to continue to be, not to perish, to last, endure, to remain as one*) in my love, just as I have kept my Father's commandments and abide in his love.

Heavenly Father, thank You that we can dwell, remain, sit, abide, have our abode, stay, lodge, sojourn, tarry, never to depart, continue to be present, held, kept continually, continue to not perish, to last, endure, live, and remain as one with You.

~ Psalm 91:1, John 15:4, John 15:10.

~ *Being Real* ~

I love my friends and those who I meet on my journey through life. Their personalities and pasts are different and unique. Some grew up in Christian homes, others did not. I'm amazed and humbled to hear their stories, to see how they found God, and where God found them.

One friend called me after she accepted Christ. The joy in her voice was obvious. I had to laugh when she let a profanity slip. The television censors wouldn't have batted an eyelash, profanity had been part of her vocabulary--she didn't even notice. But now she was truly a new creation, and I rejoiced with her.

We don't have to hide who we are or what we've done when we come to God. He already knew and already made provision for every sin. Christ takes each of us in our fallen state and creates something new. That's the neat thing—Christians aren't perfect, we serve a perfect Savior.

The Bible is full of examples about imperfect people—prostitutes, liars, adulterers, murderers, thieves, fornicators. All of them accepted and made whole through God's grace, mercy, and forgiveness.

My past is riddled with failure. But I want to be real—take what I was, and who I am now, and offer it to God to use in whatever way He sees fit. So today, please know that Christ died for you. He came to save you.

Right now, this minute, He is calling, wanting for you to come home. Dear friend, God loves you and that is real.

Heavenly Father thank You that if we confess our sins You are faithful and righteous to forgive us and cleanse us from all unrighteousness. And in Christ, we are recreated anew.~ 1 John 1:9, 2 Corinthians 5:17

~ Not Broken – Beautifully Sculpted ~

Ever wonder about the negative and/or traumatic things that happened during your life? What if we could go back and fix what went wrong? Loved ones wouldn't die. Illness wouldn't exist. Evil couldn't attack. Mistakes would be undone.

We would all be different. At very young ages several of my friends lost their mothers, and that loss deeply affected them. Now I watch as they tenderly nurture their children, family, and friends.

Many of my friends were abused and have gone through terrible difficulties. Through God's love they found healing, and now reach out to help others.

Other friends struggle with illness. Yet even with their own difficulties, they lift up others to God's throne. Some friends took very rough roads, living such wild lives their past would be too extreme to watch on evening television. Through God's grace, they walk in freedom telling others of God's forgiveness, goodness, and mercy.

There is this marvelous, mysterious, awesomeness that God takes areas of brokenness and sculpts them into something beautiful.

Through God's loving hands we aren't broken; we are beautifully, perfectly sculpted.

Heavenly Father thank You that no matter what has happened in my life, You are able to restore, redeem, and create beauty.

~ *The Great Adverbectomy* ~

When I first began writing, I wrote completely without guidance, operating my keyboard without training wheels. After several manuscript rejections, I found much-needed help through a critique group. My first writing mentor addressed a problem. Since I had enough adverbs in my first paragraph to give an editor a heart attack, they were removed. Gasp. Wheeze. Whimper. I loved my adverbs. They were astonishingly, beguilingly, charmingly, alluringly wonderful.

After recovering from shock, I went home and held a small service in their honor. Lovingly, longingly, I took one final look at my Word document before starting my search.

Weepingly, I sought for any word ending in the dreaded, tell-tale "ly" and my pages lit up like a Christmas tree. Adverbs were everywhere! No longer did they look as innocent. Goodness they had infiltrated a perfectly, decently written document and created something abnormally, agonizingly, alarmingly irritating. My work headed to the verb gym for a total manuscript makeover. Wow, who knew training could create such a lean document. Yes, the great adverbectomy was a touch painful. And although at times I may gaze longingly at my adverb buddies, in reality my manuscripts are better without them.

In the same way, there are things in our lives that we think are okay, but in reality hinder our growth as Christians. Or perhaps there are things that cause us to stumble and sin. God provides the manual – His Holy Word – to guide us along our path. We don't get to pick and choose what we think works best; we need to remember God is the creator and He has the final word on how best to live our lives.

Talk to God and ask Him to show you anything that might be holding you back. And even if it's a touch painful to remove, God wants to make sure you are the best you.

Heavenly Father show me anything in my life that is holding me back from being the best me You want me to be.

~ Work Of Art ~

My friend, Patricia, is a fused-glass artist. Sitting on my desk is a small cross that she made from seventy-five pieces of glass. Some colors change when they are fired in the furnace, so each piece was individually chosen, hand-cut, and perfectly shaped. No mold is used and no two are exactly alike. The process and product is amazing-- ordinary glass becomes a work of art.

Now I could take those same pieces of glass and formulate an absolute mess. But from the hands of an artist, comes beauty.

God paints the sky, tints the ocean, colors the flowers, and creates beauty for us to enjoy every day. He also created each of us— individually, no two alike. Within each of us are pieces of good and bad memories, events, and influences.

I didn't want any of the "bad" pieces. I wanted to hide them away, throw them out, and pretend they didn't exist. Fortunately I can ask for forgiveness for the bad things I have done. But what can be done with all the pain and suffering caused by others?

Remember those glass pieces which are one color before firing and another color after? God is the artist. He takes our messed up lives, mends our wounds, restores, and renews. His unfailing love fires through and He creates beauty.

In His hands we will always be a work of art.

Heavenly Father thank You that everything is beautiful in Your hands and in Your timing. ~ Ecclesiastes 3:11

~ Scared Barkless ~

Our little dog loves to stand on the window seat of my office and watch out the front window. In his mind, his job is to protect our home from all invaders – especially those with four legs and fur. For a little guy, his bark gets rather deep when another dog dares to stroll by on the sidewalk.

When the street sweeper rumbled past on the street outside, the sound reverberated in the room. Our dog stood his ground but couldn't find his bark. All he could do was watch and shake. Poor baby. I went to his side, told him everything would be okay, and tried to provide comfort. Those puppy eyes searched mine, but he still shook.

He'll be okay. I know. I have knowledge that he doesn't.

Sometimes I stand my ground, bark at problems and the enemy with gusto. Other times, all I can do is whimper.

Through God's word I find comfort. God knows things I don't know. He knows yesterday, today, and tomorrow. He has knowledge I don't have. Thankfully, God hears, understands, and never leaves our side—even when we're scared barkless.

Heavenly Father, thank You for Your protection. Thank You that Your Spirit intercedes for us even when we are too scared to speak.

~ Rest? ~

My mornings are often a struggle—I want to get out of bed early, beat the world to the punch, and check off that I have accomplished mighty things for God and His Kingdom. Don't ask me what I think I'll do, I just want to do something.

Instead, a still small voice in my spirit tells me to be still, cease striving, and rest. Rest? Argh! Who has time for rest?

I've rested enough while I struggled eleven years with Lyme Disease. So I toss and turn, try to pray, pray, try to rest, read scripture, try to read scripture, check my emails on my phone, check the time, toss and turn, and try to rest. When I get out of bed exhausted, then rush through my day worried I may have missed something.

A sweet friend put things into proper perspective; she said to relentlessly pursue not hurrying. I love that concept. Happy sigh.

I don't have to go through life in such a rush. I can slow down, rest when God says to rest, and take a deep breath.

Want to join me? You won't even have to run to catch up. I'll be strolling along life's trail enjoying what God wants me to enjoy.

Heavenly Father thank You for rest. Help me not to fight the wonderful gift You give us as we rest in You. I'm taking a deep breath and curling up in Your presence.

~ Innocence Restored ~

The Old Idaho State Penitentiary first opened its doors in 1870 and continued to operate until 1973. During the years of operation housed 13,000 convicts, one of which was Harry Orchard. Orchard began his sentence in 1908 after being convicted of the assassination of a former governor of Idaho. Years later, due to good behavior, Orchard was offered parole. He chose to stay and eventually died on April 13, 1954. Our tour guide surmised perhaps the man had enemies on the outside he didn't want to face, or after serving so long in prison, he couldn't imagine leaving.

After parole was offered, Harry chose to return to his dingy cell, never again to experience freedom. He had a choice. We also have a choice.

Many people are locked in their past. Their innocence was taken from them, or through their own bad choices innocence was lost. Unable to move forward, they remain trapped in the prison of their mind. Memories pounce and mangle leaving us shaking, quaking, unable to process what happened, much less deal with today.

How can we regain what was lost? How can we go free when our enemies continue to roam, or our own failures condemn us? The enemy pushes us inside the prison but can't lock us in. Jesus stands at the door to our freedom. He came to set the captives free and to release the prisoners, Luke 4:18. And if we choose freedom, we go through Christ to be washed clean. Innocence is regained, and what was once lost is restored.

Please visualize the process. God offers total and complete restoration. You chose Christ. Every bad thought, every evil action and every evil touch, taken away. Every bit of sin is forgiven and removed. Every spot now pure. You are wholly recreated in Christ. When God looks at you, He sees His perfect Son.

Your prison cell is open and you are free. Again, Jesus stands at the door, this time to block the path back to the past.

Those bad memories? You don't have to go back, Jesus stands at the door. Those failures? They're gone, Jesus stands at the door. Your sins? They're clean, Jesus stands at the door. Don't listen to Satan's lies that you can never be free, or your innocence never regained.

Don't believe the enemy who was behind all the evil in the first place. The cell door is open and Jesus stands at the door.

In Christ, you are completely, totally, washed clean, innocence restored, recreated and free.

God's word blesses us with wonderful passages on freedom, please read Psalm 68:6, Psalm 68:20, Psalm 146:7, Galatians 5:1, Isaiah 1:18, Psalm 103:11, and Psalm 56:13.

~ Time-Out ~

God gently said it's time—time for a time out from the busyness of life, and time for time in with Him. Ulcers, headaches, and stress were signs that something was wrong. And what was wrong was me. I was so busy with all I felt called to do, that I wasn't staying plugged into The One who made the call.

I closed down one of my most active social sites, and although I miss the online interaction, I desperately missed God's presence more. Nothing I write, say, post, or blog will have any value unless it comes from God. No offering is worthy without God's blessing. I can't save anyone, but I can point to The Savior – Jesus Christ.

Psalm 119 voices my prayer.

I have gone astray like a lost sheep, seek Your servant... Teach me, Lord... Revive me according to Your word ... Open my eyes that I may see wonderful things from Your law ... I will speak of Your testimonies ... Your word has revived me ... Teach me good discernment and knowledge ... Give me understanding ... Your word is a lamp to my feet and a light to my path ... I am Your servant ... Establish my footsteps ... I rejoice at Your word ... You are my hiding place ... Let my tongue sing at Your word ... Let my lips utter praise ... Your law is my delight ... I have inclined my heart to perform Your statutes forever, even to the end ... For I do not forget Your commandments.

I love You, Father. My time is Yours, and I am Yours forever.

~ No Fear ~

I've been pondering 2 Timothy 1:7. God hasn't given us the spirit of fear, but gives us power, love, and a sound mind. A tiny verse with so much meat.

Fear – God did NOT give us the spirit of fear. We don't have to live under what is identified as cowardice, craven/cringing fear, fawning fear, timidity, or gnawing fear. God gives us a courageous spirit – His Spirit!

Power – Strength and ability, dynamite power, courageous in difficulties and dangers. God's power – miraculous, nothing-is-impossible power encompassing heaven and earth. Power without fear.

Love – God's love for His people. Love that seeks above self to focus on the glory of God and the interests of Christ and the good of souls. Love that will carry us through any opposition we may meet, setting us above the fear of man. A Spirit of fired-up-love, inflaming us to minister in God's service, loving freely with His love. Love without fear.

Sound Mind – Self-control, discipline, calm, well-balanced mind, a quietness of mind centered on God's truth. A sound mind without fear. Woo hoo! Allow God's truth to wash over you. NO fear!

Let's live the NO fear, God-given fearless life.

Heavenly Father, thank You that in You we have nothing to fear. Thank You for Your power, love, and that we can center our mind on You and Your truth. Help me to live forever fearlessly fearless in You.

~ Porch Sitting ~

I had been a bear for weeks. Distance seemed to separate me from God as I worried and fretted. My husband's layoff was coming, my health again seemed fragile, and I wondered what would happen in the future. Would we move once again? Would the stress of job, school, and health continue?

I had quite the pity party, snapping at my family, sitting in my office chair, and feeling quite the martyr. Whimper, whine, and moan, please stop the world, I want to get off.

Then during my quiet time, I read about the joy of being in the presence of Jesus. Joy comes by abiding in His presence because everything else fades. Worries vanish, stress abates, and joy returns.

I pictured sitting on the front porch of a cabin in the woods, the porch high enough I can sit on the edge and dangle my feet. The weather is perfect and the scenery beautiful. Next to me is Jesus, and He's smiling. The past, present, and future, disappear in the light of His presence. I am immersed in pure joy.

And the wonderful thing is, Jesus wants to spend time with us and delights in His children. And in His joy we realize that God's grace, mercy, joy, guidance, comfort, peace, provision, healing, strength, and unfailing love keeps us safe forever.

Join me on the porch, there's plenty of room. Dangle your feet, look into your Savior's eyes, and experience His joy.

You will make known to me the path of life; In Your presence is fullness of joy; In Your right hand there are pleasures forever. ~ Psalm 16:11 NASB

~ Fear Imps ~

I hesitate to admit I have fearful moments. As a Christian, shouldn't I always be brave and strong in God? Thankfully, God loves us even with our human frailties. He gave us a working mind and emotions. Fear in itself is not a negative. Without fear I would be jumping off mountains or body surfing a waterfall. Healthy fear keeps me out of trouble and gives a proper perspective on reality. The problem comes when fear becomes bigger than the belief in God's sovereignty, love, protection, and provision.

The other morning fear, worry, and anxiety clawed and clung to my shoulders. I hurried to my study, clicked on the Bible software, and searched for verses on fear. As I scrolled and read through God's word, those nasty fear imps dropped off my shoulders and vaporized.

Hebrews 4:12 tells us that God's word is living and active, and sharper than any double-edged sword. Dear one, draw your sword and stand on His promises. You never battle alone.

Fear not. Don't be afraid. Say to those with fearful hearts, I am with you. I have heard your cry. I love you. Perfect love casts out fear. Don't be dismayed. Don't be discouraged. I will help you. I have redeemed you. I have summoned you by name. I will save you. I am your shield. I will protect you. I am your deliverer. I will go with you. I will fight for you. I will defend you. I will never leave you. I will strengthen you and help you. I will support you with my right hand. I have heard your prayer. Take courage, take heart, I am here! For nothing is impossible with God.

Don't be afraid, I've redeemed you. I've called your name. You're mine. When you're in over your head, I'll be there with you. When you're in rough waters, you will not go down. When you're between a rock and a hard place, it won't be a dead end—Because I am God, your personal God, The Holy One of Israel, your Savior. ~ Isaiah 43:1-4 MSG

~ Don't Miss The Blessings ~

My head pounded with a raging migraine. Slumped in the recliner with light-blocking eye mask over my eyes, blankets to warm me, and the Christian music channel playing whisper-soft songs, I prayed for relief.

The next morning, hubby's alarm went off at his usual time at 5:15. I stayed in bed reading devotions and praying. Snuggled in my covers, I prayed God would direct my day.

Then, I sensed His still small voice, *Get out of the bed. Don't miss the blessing.*

Surely, I imagined it. Would God answer my prayer that quickly? Maybe it was just me thinking I needed to get up. Again, I prayed.

The soft voice whispered once more in my spirit, *Don't miss the blessing.*

Maybe I could sleep a little longer and still get the blessing?

Insistent, the words beckoned, *Don't miss the blessing.* No condemnation, more a gentle, smiling prod.

My curiosity piqued, I relented. I took a shower and prepared for the day. Convinced God would bless me with a fabulous sunrise, I grabbed my camera and Bible. With a cup of hot tea, I settled in a chair at the kitchen table and opened the blinds.

Blackness greeted me. I sipped my tea, read my Bible, and kept an eye on the view outside. The sky began its gradual lightening. No colors. Nothing special, only gray clouds.

I tucked away my camera. And then it occurred to me, my quiet time of reading had been a blessing. A blessing I would have missed staying in bed.

My son thumped down the stairs. He hadn't felt well for several days and still was dragging. Since I had been up early, breakfast awaited him. I enjoyed getting to visit—definitely another blessing.

Then I remembered a Christian music site we had discussed. Earlier he had some problems accessing it, and we were able to finally get things working. He was thrilled finding music suited to his style with Christian lyrics. Oh my, now that was a wonderful blessing! I watched his awesome smile and reveled in his excitement.

In those moments, I realized the blessings weren't earth shattering, and not what I expected, but they filled my heart with joy. God has blessings waiting for each of us. God's blessings, bless us, and bless others.

Today and every day watch with excitement, and whatever you do, don't miss the blessings.

~ Surprised, But Not Forsaken ~

Ever had one of those days where you felt like you were driving in perfect weather, enjoying life, when all of the sudden the wheels fall off and you are left sitting in the middle of the road wondering what happened?

A few years ago everything was right with the world. We had a contract on our Texas house and a contract on a new home in Idaho. The pack and move dates were set and my flight arranged for the closing and move.

Then we got the call.

Our Texas buyers backed out twelve hours before they would lose their earnest money and thirteen days before closing. If we didn't close on the Idaho house, we would lose $2000.00 earnest money. Then, my health tanked.

So we sat and wondered. We had prayed every step of the way and seemed to have God's blessings. What happened? I kept thinking of the verse in Jeremiah 29:11, God knows the plans He has for us. Plans to prosper and not harm, plans for hope and a future.

We truly believed His promises. And even though we whined and cried, we knew everything would work out. Although we lost our earnest money, and waited many more months before the Texas house would sell, God provided. And we moved into a new home, better than the one we had originally wanted.

No matter what twists and turns life may take, God is always in control. He knows the plan for our very best today and our very best tomorrow. The days might not be easy, we can't see in the future, but we can be assured God is never surprised and we are never forsaken.

Thank You, Father for wild rides. Thank You, that You are always in control. Take me off-road or through twists and turns—anything that brings me closer to You.

~ View Check~

One weekend, sweet hubby and I decided to travel to the Idaho Sawtooth Mountains. Oh my goodness, what a gorgeous drive. Snow has such a peaceful, quiet, calming quality—especially when you are nice and toasty in the car.

The snow seemed to lessen as we drove farther and turned toward Sun Valley. Although absolutely gorgeous, I still expected to see more snow (even if it was in March).

We kept driving, stopping to take photos, and finally decided to return home. The most amazing thing happened when we turned in the new direction. The snow was deeper. One side of the mountain would be almost bare, and the other side was covered in layers of white beauty.

The deep snow had always been there. Nothing had changed but my view.

Some days our problems look deep and unending. Other times life is barren and dry. However one thing never changes – God. Regardless of our limited earthly view, God is always faithful, always true, always merciful, and always loving.

Thank You Heavenly Father that You know the paths we take. You know the future and You know the way. Regardless of what the road looks like ahead, help me to keep my view on You.

~ *Through* ~

God's word promises, no matter what you are going through, God will help you through. Even when we walk through the valley of the shadow of death, He is with us. His plans stand firm forever through all generations.

Through Him, we push back enemies and trample foes. His paths leads through seas and mighty waters. For the Lord is good and His love endures faithfully forever through all generations. When we pass through the waters, He will be with us. When we pass through the rivers, they won't sweep over us. When we walk through the fire, we won't be burned, the flames will not set us ablaze.

This is what the Lord says—He who made a way through the sea, a path through the mighty waters, forget the former things, don't dwell on the past, I'm doing new things and making a way in the desert and streams in the wasteland.

I will go before you and level mountains, break down the gates of bronze and cut through bars of iron. Since we have been justified through faith, we have peace with God through our Lord Jesus Christ, through whom we have gained access by faith. We are more than conquerors through Him who loved us. Praise God, He gives victory through our Lord Jesus Christ.

Through Christ our comfort overflows. In Him and through faith in Him we may approach God with freedom and confidence. For no matter how many promises God has made, they are "Yes" in Christ. And so through Him the "Amen" is spoken by us to the glory of God. Such confidence as this is ours through Christ before God.

I pray that out of His glorious riches He may strengthen you with power through His Spirit in your inner being. I can do everything through Him who gives me strength. He is able to save completely those who come to God through Him, because He always lives to intercede for them.

May God himself, the God of peace, sanctify you through and through. May your whole spirit, soul and body be kept blameless at the coming of our Lord Jesus Christ.

Heavenly Father, thank You for the truth found in Your word. Help me to remember no matter what I'm going through You are there to help me through.

~ Psalm 23:4, Psalm 33:11, Psalm 44:5, Psalm 77:19, Psalm 100:5, Isaiah 43:2, Isaiah 43:16,18-19, Isaiah 45:2, Romans 5:1-2, Romans 8:37, 1 Corinthians 15:57, 2 Corinthians 1:5, Ephesians 3:12, 2 Corinthians 1:20, 2 Corinthians 3:4, Ephesians 3:16, Philippians 4:13, Hebrews 7:25, 1 Thessalonians 5:23.

~ I Can't ~

For thirty-eight years a man had waited for healing. And then Jesus walks into his life, "Do you want to get well?"

The man's response... "I can't, sir, for I have no one to put me into the pool when the water bubbles up. Someone else always gets there ahead of me." ~ John 5:7 NLT

The man never replied to the question, he only gave excuses and reasons for his continued condition.

Is God asking you to trust Him, to move outside your comfort zone, to believe the impossible? Can you only see the excuses and obstacles? Is God asking you to do something you don't think you can do, something that seems beyond your comprehension?

Will you believe God, The One Who created all things, The One Who can do all things. Will you believe enough to say, "Yes Lord, I can and will believe all things are possible with You."

Heavenly Father I never want to say "I can't" to You, because nothing is impossible for You. Help me to believe and trust in Your power, might, love, and grace to know that I can do all things through Christ who strengthens me.

~ Forever Safe ~

In the study, *Scouting the Divine* by Margaret Feinberg, the second session records a current-day shepherdess and the relationship with one of her ill sheep. She had summoned a vet, administered medicine, all with concern and compassion. The love and devotion of the shepherdess brought tears to my eyes as I pictured God's tender care as The Great Shepherd.

I picture God comforting His children through difficulties. I think of friends who battle devastating diseases—the e-mails and quiet conversations discussing the horrors of illness and yet the awestruck amazement that in their darkest moments they feel the presence of God.

I consider the precious women God has brought into my life. Some walk close to the Shepherd and hang on His every word. Others roam the pasture not quite sure where they fit in the fold. Many stay outside God's care, not truly believing He is trustworthy or He will somehow keep them from experiencing all they desire. And within all of them is a hunger to be known and loved.

Wolves are in the world, storms will come, rivers are swift, and fires sweep over the open range. Yet those who follow God, The Great Shepherd, will guide you safely through every dark valley. No wolf can snatch you from His care. He'll keep your head afloat when you pass through raging rivers. In the fires He will shield you from the flames. And when death comes, He'll guide you home—forever safe.

Heavenly Father, thank You that You are the Good Shepherd and we are forever safe in Your loving hands.

~ Psalm 23:4, Isaiah 43:2, John 10:27-29.

~ Pedaling Or Powering ~

I wonder how often I am truly aware of God's power. I sit in my little proverbial push car, wearing myself out, determined to use all my strength and muscle my way through life. Ignoring, or only vaguely acknowledging that God grants His power and His strength. The God Who took nothing and made everything. The God Who knows the name of every star too numerous to count. The God Who offers eternal life.

Hmmm… I think I'll park the pedal car.

I pray that out of His glorious riches he will strengthen you with power through His Spirit, so Christ may dwell in your hearts through faith. And I pray that you being rooted and established in love, may have power to grasp how wide, long, high, and deep the love of Christ is, that you may be filled with the fullness of God. God is able to do more than we can ask or imagine according to His power at work within us. ~ Ephesians 3:16-21

~ *The Power Of One* ~

Without my tethering to my creator God, I'm nothing but a puff of dust blowing across the planet. I'm absolutely completely miserable if I don't read, speak, or write of my Lord. I can't hold His word inside.

I desperately feed on God's word, books, devotions, and blogs that drive me deeper into His heart. There is this burning desire to share with others about our wonderful God. A God who knows the stars by name, yet sings over us lowly earth creatures, even knowing the hairs on our heads. A God who is kind, merciful, loving, and compassionate. A God who through nail-scarred hands offers forgiveness and eternal life.

How could I not share this wonderful truth and joy? How can I keep silent about this amazing treasure? I pound away day after day at my keyboard weaving God's truth into blogs, articles, and manuscripts.

Why can't I tell the whole world? Why can't I share God's truth with those who have no pillow for their heads, or those who are suffering at the hands of evil? Why can't I tell the lonely they are forever loved? Why can't I share with the lost that they can be found?

I'm only one person, but God, amazing, universe-creating God, has other children. They too can tell. They too can speak.

For then the power of one becomes the power of THE ONE.

Please share with others. Tell the world, that each one can tell another one so that all can connect to The One.

Who is like the LORD our God, the One who sits enthroned on high. ~ *Psalm 113:5 NIV*

~ *Boom Where You're Planted* ~

I love Spring! The flowers bloom, trees bud and blossom, and the birds sing melodies. But what happens if a bud doesn't bud? Will it remain a bud, enfolded in beauty, or eventually just wither?

And I wonder, am I blossoming in the many aspects of life? Am I flourishing or withering?

The areas of my life where I enfold on myself, at first seem fine, but eventually wither. The areas I give freely to God blossom and flourish.

I don't know about you, but I want to live beyond the bud.

And what if we truly lived in God's strength and energy? Would we merely be a small bloom on the end of His living vine? Or would we explode with His power?

Father, help me to live beyond the bud, blooming and booming with Your power wherever You plant me. Help me to fully open my heart to You, that I may blossom under Your loving care.

~ *Human Target* ~

Would I live differently if I knew I had a 24/7 bodyguard? You betcha! Man, I'd be fearless. Regardless of where I went and what I did, someone would always be there for my protection.

A television show ran for several season called, Human Target. The information read: "It takes a brave, selfless man to make himself a 'human target' in order to save the lives of those in danger. For Chance, it's about one thing only: saving his clients' lives."

Interesting idea. Perhaps the premise sounds familiar?

Christopher Chance is only a television character. Jesus Christ is real. When the punishment required for our sin meant death (being eternally separated from God), Jesus became the target in our place. When we chose to believe in Him, we are placed under His protection, and our souls are eternally safe.

Isn't that awesome! We have a 24/7 soul bodyguard.

Thank You, Jesus for becoming the human target for my sin. Please help me to live each day soul confident and fearless in You.

Jesus gave his life for our sins, just as God our Father planned, in order to rescue us from this evil world in which we live. Therefore he is able, once and forever, to save those who come to God through him. He lives forever to intercede with God on their behalf. ~ Galatians 1:4 NLT, Hebrews 7:25 NLT

~ For Such A Time As This ... So That ~

God's word is amazing. Did you know you were born for such a time as this? There is a time to be born and a time to die and God determined the times set for us and the exact places that we should live.

And that's just part of the amazing picture. With every, for such a time as this, there is a, so that. We are here so that our purposes are fulfilled and to bring God glory. We are called to love and obey God so that people will know we are His disciples.

Repent/Confess/Forgive so that sins may be wiped out, refreshing may come, we're forgiven and the enemy can't get an advantage.

Ask so that it will be given, that workers will be sent into the harvest, and the Son may bring glory to the Father. Obey so that you may be successful, careful to do what God calls you to do, abiding in His love, joy and delight.

Trials and perseverance are so that you are tested and kept from sinning and the work of God may be displayed in your life. And so that your faith is purified resulting in praise, glory, and honor for God. And so that you may be mature, complete, and not lacking in anything.

We are comforted so that we may comfort others. We are told to come/abide/remain in Christ so that we will bear fruit and find rest. Give so that you may respect God, receive His pressed down, shaken together, running over rewards.

Live Godly lives so that it will go well with you, showing you are a child of God, with a new life, bearing fruit, bringing praise to God, overflowing with hope, filled with the full measure of all the fullness of God, blessed with knowing God better, having fellowship with one another, and walking in His ways.

Jesus came into the world so that we might have eternal, full, light-filled life. And let your light shine so that others can see God's light and receive forgiveness of sins.

Search for yourself and ponder all the wonderful ways God works for such a time as this and the resulting so that!

Thank You Heavenly Father, that every step I take, every path You lay in front of me is for such a time as this, so that Your purposes may be fulfilled. And Your purposes and plans are the best! Use me for such a time as this, so that You may be glorified.

~ For I Know The Plans ~

I'm having bunches of fun with my Bible study. I'm researching and studying the meanings of words using the Bible, Webster's dictionary, Bible study references, and Greek and Hebrew definitions.

I examined one of my favorite verses, Jeremiah 29:11 in different translations.

For I know the plans I have for you, declares the LORD, plans to prosper you and not to harm you, plans to give you hope and a future. ~ Jeremiah 29:11 NIV.

For I know the plans I have for you, says the Lord. They are plans for good and not for disaster, to give you a future and a hope. ~ Jeremiah 29:11 NLT.

For I know the thoughts and plans that I have for you, says the Lord, thoughts and plans for welfare and peace and not for evil, to give you hope in your final outcome. ~ Jeremiah 29:11 AMP.

Some of the definitions are:

Plans = Thought, design, purpose, to determine. A series of steps to be carried out or goals to be accomplished.

Prosper = Peace, safety, prosperity, well-being, intactness, wholeness. Peace can have a focus of security, safety which can bring feelings of satisfaction, well-being, and contentment.

Hope = The general feeling that some desire will be fulfilled. Expect with desire.

God has a design. He knows the steps that need to be taken to carry out the ultimate goal for our lives. His plan is good, peaceful, safe, prosperous, leads to well-being, wholeness, and contentment. His plan is not evil, harmful or disastrous. His plan gives a desirous expectation in our final, future outcome.

Isn't that neat? Treasures are just waiting to be found.

Pray and ask for understanding as you dig deeper with God and His word, and enjoy the amazing depths and treasures of His love.

~ Borrowing Trouble ~

I'm worried. My mind races to prepare for every aspect of what life might throw my way. I hate that. I shouldn't be worried. I shouldn't worry about what might happen, or the what-if's, or about tomorrow. I know what I should do, lay all my cares and worries at the feet of the cross. Instead, I go around borrowing trouble.

Excuse me sir, may I have a cup of trouble? I'm running low today, and when tomorrow comes I might not be prepared.

Argh! What on earth am I thinking?

Maybe that's the problem, I'm thinking from an earthly perspective.

God's grace is always available. He will provide for every need. His grace is big enough to handle any problem, any worry, any what-if, and every tomorrow.

Heavenly Father, help me to not borrow trouble but always rest in Your precious grace. Let me fearlessly, confidently, and boldly draw near to Your throne of grace to find grace for each and every need. ~ Hebrews 4:16

~ Never Useless ~

Illness stinks, long-term illness . . . well, it stinks even more. It's bad enough being sick, but then there is that nagging worry about not doing anything worthwhile. Being useless. Groan. Whimper.

Fortunately we are never useless. Everyone has a purpose in God's kingdom. God doesn't define us by what we can do, but what we will allow Him to do through us. God is not impressed by physical strength. He only asks we trust Him and place our faith in His strength and His might. Paul shared that in his weakness God was strong. And fortunately God does not look at outward strength; He looks at inner strength. And inner strength is freely supplied by Him in limitless quantity.

God gives strength to his people. He gives strength to the weary and increases the power of the weak ~ Psalm 29:11, Isaiah 40:29.

Strange as it may sound, some of my best times were when I was too ill and weak to do anything but lay in bed talking to God. In the darkness, God's light shined all the brighter. And in those moments, I learned that regardless of circumstances, we're never useless. Every breath taken has a purpose.

What a blessing that no matter where we are physically, we can focus on God who makes all things possible. We can spend time with Him, pray, read His word, and get to know His heart. We can be available to others. For in encouraging others we find encouragement. Even when our world is shaken, we can find strength in God's solid foundation.

Heavenly Father, let us rise like a phoenix above the ashes of life's circumstances, leaving a trail for others to follow straight to heaven's door.

~ Invincible! ~

I've had my wimpy, whiny, and weak moments. I pictured removing my outer, saggy, skin layer and dragging my woeful little body down the hall. Goodness I miss the days I could lift more weight than several of the body builders in our gym. I was woman, hear me roar. Now I am woman, hear me whine.

The world can be a tough and rough place, and it's hard sometimes to be brave. However as followers of Christ, we don't have to live in fear. We may live in a fallen world with falling bodies, but our inner soul is being renewed day by day. As Christians, we will live forever in the happily-ever-after. We get new bodies and are invincible in Christ.

Soooo as an invincible, shouldn't we be living an invincible life?

Let's live life to the fullest, speaking boldly and telling others about The One who offers forgiveness, grace, and mercy. Jesus Christ gives strength to the weary, turns mourning into joy, and death into life eternal. No more hiding in fear, no more worrying about tomorrow, no more timidity.

Through Christ, we are invincible. Let's be invincible followers telling others about our invincible Savior!

May our Lord Jesus Christ himself and God our Father, who loved us and by his grace gave us eternal encouragement and good hope, encourage your hearts and strengthen you in every good deed and word. He saved us, not because of righteous things we had done, but because of his mercy. He saved us through the washing of rebirth and renewal by the Holy Spirit, whom he poured out on us generously through Jesus Christ our Savior, so that, having been justified by his grace, we might become heirs having the hope of eternal life.~ 2 Thessalonians 2:16-17, Titus 3:5-7, NIV.

~ Healing Memories ~

I was eighteen, in a hospital, and left alone with a male radiation technician. I was strapped down and put in a horrific situation which was witnessed by someone else who walked in the room. I still see the young man's shocked expression. Time froze as our eyes met, and he left before being seen by the technician. To cope, I locked the door on that memory.

The scene replayed, and I was faced with a choice. Would I allow the tail-spin, the heavy cloak of emotions, and the mental wound examination? I didn't want to go there. I want to always walk in freedom. I tried to read God's word looking for answers, but sometimes even focusing on the word is tough.

A song came to mind by Scott Krippayne, "*You are Still God.*" Yet for some reason my computer music library only contained part of the song. I clicked over to an online music service, and while I was waiting for the upload, four songs were suggested. I usually ignore their recommendations, but this time, I listened. And while I listened, God's truth poured out healing.

For in song we often find God's truth and comfort. We are made for praise. Praise loosens and frees us from the enemy's hold and plugs us back into God's power and strength. Praise soothes and settles a soul. Praise takes our eyes off the past and moves us forward. Praise heals. Praise is a wonderful blessing. If you are dealing with issues in your past, turn on the praise.

Heavenly Father, I don't understand why some things happen, but I do know You are always in control and You shield my soul. Nothing takes You by surprise, the times when fear clutches me, I can speak the name of Jesus and rise up in freedom. All my chains are stripped away, and my heart sings praises as I live and rest in the victory Christ won for me. Father, I pray for both men. I pray for the one who did wrong that he will repent and come to know You. I also pray for the young man who was a witness, please heal his memories and don't allow the enemy to use that in negative ways. I give the memory to You and rest in the knowledge and freedom of Your love. I am free!

~ Hip Hydraulics ~

Thanks to football and marathon running, my sweet hubby had both his hips replaced. Yes, I am married to the bionic man—he is stronger, faster, and definitely more expensive. Our son suggested making the surgeries more worthwhile by ordering accessories; perhaps hydraulics, or a built in MP3 player. Don't worry, we didn't ask the surgeon.

Hubby's bad hip was replaced and his pain gone. Other than the initial sore thigh from the eight inch titanium spike. Amazing what the medical community can do these days. I am grateful.

Surgeons can replace, stitch, and mend, but God is in the restoration business. Whether the wounds are heart or flesh, God knows what is needed to heal. There is no injury too large, and no hurt beyond His healing touch.

Got pain?

God is the answer.

And after you have suffered a little while, the God of all grace, who has called you to his eternal glory in Christ, will himself restore, confirm, strengthen, and establish you. ~ 1 Peter 5:10 ESV

~ Wagging ~

In my humble opinion, we have the cutest dog on the whole planet. He's a sixteen pound bundle of fur who loves to bark at the squirrels who run across the top of our fence. When tired, our pup carries his blanket in his mouth, fluffs it until he finds the perfect spot and nurses until he goes to sleep.

He absolutely loves receiving gifts. He will dance on his hind legs and wag for a full hour if we bring him a new toy or chew bone. The floor next to my desk is littered with dog toys, I can't help it, I love to bring him gifts. How can I refuse when he is so appreciative?

I watch him, and I wonder if I'm as appreciative with God when He blesses me so abundantly. I have a wonderful husband and son, neat family and friends, great church, and the list continues until I would run out of room. I'm also thankful for the negative things in my life because they helped make me who I am today. And I wouldn't change a thing because through the hardships, failures, and difficulties, I have discovered more of God.

Dear Heavenly Father, thank You. Thank You for today. Let me dance for joy for the abundant gifts you give each day. If I had a tail, it would wag. Help me to bring joy to You Father. Even when things are not going well, even when sick, even though life is painful, help me to remember to praise You. For I have life everlasting, and one day I will see Your face and dance on the streets of gold praising You. Thank You Father, Thank You! Praise You forever Father. In the precious Name of Your Son, Jesus Christ, who is my Savior and Redeemer, Amen

~ Difficulties ~

After years of weird health problems, I'm used to the tests and the next diagnosis. How grateful I am for a God who guides, loves, and provides for every need.

God has taken away unexplained knots, cysts, illnesses, and miraculously healed tumors. He has gently walked me through surgeries, difficulties, and the ongoing Lyme disease. I'm so blessed, but it doesn't mean life is not hard. I strive to walk in His presence and couldn't take a step without Him.

God knows how we feel. He wants honesty. Goodness, He knows every thought. When morning comes and sleep has been difficult, when uncertainty looms ahead, we can crawl into His arms and make it another day. In Him, we find help for the day knowing He is in control. He will be with us and provide for every need.

He loves you. No matter what you are facing, no matter what you have been through, where you have come from, and no matter what tomorrow brings. He is near. He is here. He is at every point of need.

Ah Lord God! Behold, You have made the heavens and the earth by Your great power and by Your outstretched arm! Nothing is too difficult for You. ~ Jeremiah 32:17 NASB

~ Wake-Up Call ~

My first years as a stay-at-home mom left me drained and exhausted. When our son, Scott finally started sleeping through the night, he rose before dawn, wide-eyed and eager for the day. I begged God, "Please make him stay asleep longer." Poor little guy did not have a sweet mommy when he bounded on my bed in the mornings.

Getting tired of my own pity-parties, I knew I desperately needed quiet moments before the day began. Finally God broke through my stubborn streak reminding me I could get up earlier. Determined to get a jump on our boundless energy-filled son, I moved the coffee pot to the bathroom and rose at 5:30 am.

Java in hand and Bible open, I had plenty of time to spend with God before Scott charged through the door. Focusing on God first thing, helped my attitude, feelings, and perspective for the day change for the better. I'm sure Scott was amazed at how much nicer his mom had become.

Scott never waned in his excitement, even with a cranky mom. No wonder Jesus tells us to become like children. Wouldn't it be fun to be like children and greet the day with eagerness and anticipation? The adult in me rebels, remembering the million-and-one things that I "need" to do and should take into consideration by worrying. Ah, but the child nudges me. Jesus said not to worry about tomorrow, or worry about what I'll eat or drink, or even what I'll wear. He has me covered in His love.

Jesus tells us to seek first His kingdom and righteousness and He'll take care of the rest ~ Matthew 6:33. When I keep my focus on God and seek the things that please Him, my life honestly is great. I don't have to worry because God will take care of my every need.

Goodness, if I approached life like a child, my feet would hit the floor and I'd race to explore my new day. No time for pity-parties or sleeping away mornings, I'm waking up to enjoy God and enjoy life!

Heavenly Father, Your little child is here and ready to play. Show me what You want me to do today and help me keep my child-like eyes open to watch You work and move!

~ *Whine And Cheese* ~

For a number of years, health problems have plagued a friend of mine. The doctors finally diagnosed Nancy with a disease I cannot pronounce, much less write. During a phone call, we updated one another on our ongoing medical conditions. She was beginning a new round of medication and knew the side effects would be difficult — puffiness, hair loss, nausea, and other nastiness.

I was well on my way to a major pity party of my own after surgery on shredded tendons and ligaments on my leg. The first week had been tolerable thanks to massive doses of narcotics dispensed through the pain pump tethered to my leg. But now, with the pump removed, the excruciating pain had returned. We both knew God would help us through, but the whine was strong.

Nancy: Let's do a whine and cheese party.

Lisa: Can't do cheese, I'm lactose intolerant – that would be a big whine. How about chocolate instead?

Nancy: Oh great! Okay, let's get together and have coffee at Starbucks too!

Lisa: Great, a whine, coffee and chocolate party. Problem is I still can't drive.

Nancy: I can drive. I'll come get you.

Lisa: Great. But who will help us with our wheelchairs?

Pause...

Nancy: Oh that's right. No problem, I can walk a bit, we can park close to the door.

Lisa: Okay, maybe I can use my walker and leave the wheelchair.

Nancy: I know ... we can call our friend Cherie to drive us.

Lisa: Yep, we can even buy her some coffee and chocolate.

Nancy: Yes, a baby-sitting fee.

Pause...

Laughter, side-splitting laughter. Tear-flowing, God-healing laughter, taking us from pity party to laugh party. God allowed us to whine for a time, but a good laugh gave us the perspective we needed.

God knows our situations and knows that life is often difficult. He is a loving Father, and He gives us time to grieve, and process. He promises that He has good plans to give us a hope and a future. He hears our cries, He knows our hurts, and each day He will carry us safe and secure in His tender arms.

Nancy and I never did make the Starbucks run, but we did have some fun wheelchair races at a Mexican restaurant in the following months. So once again today, I will try and leave the whine behind, and remember His precious promises to carry us through any difficulty.

When you pass through the waters, I will be with you; and when you pass through the rivers, they will not sweep over you. When you walk through the fire, you will not be burned; the flames will not set you ablaze. For I am the LORD, your God, the Holy One of Israel, your Savior. ~ Isaiah 43:2-3 NIV

~ *Whee Bump!* ~

We lived in Houston during several of my younger years. Houston terrain is flat, flatter, and flattest. The only "hills" are overpasses on the interstate.

One street near our house had a fun feature – a rolling bump. Not a speed bump, just a small rise and dip. When our car drove over the exciting anomaly (yes, we were easily entertained) it produced a momentary sinking feeling that resulted in smiles and giggles. The bump was aptly named the "Wheee bump," and that bump made the journey worthwhile.

Flat roads are rather monotonous—nothing interesting, just miles and miles of smooth, even, dreary roads.

Yawn.

Life's highways are full of curves, hair-pin turns, broken glass, and steep climbs. Many days, I longed for a boring ride. However looking back on my journey, every rough patch, screaming drop, and miles of rocky terrain brought me closer to God.

I've had some terrible moments and ongoing difficulties, but all those bumps make the story worth telling. I can show my fellow travelers that God is a God of compassion, love, mercy, grace, and healing. With His touch, everything the enemy tried to destroy has been redeemed and restored.

Whether your trip is filled with wheee bumps or dangerous travels, you're never on the adventure alone. You may have some hair-stand-on-end moments, and the stomach may drop a bit, but every mile will be filled with awesome true-life stories of God's faithfulness.

Heavenly Father I love the whee-bump journey with You!

~ Self Stewing ~

How often do we refuse to move forward? We get rutted and trapped in the past, clinging to the thing that destroyed the life we wanted or imagined.

There is a time to mourn and weep, but we've turned it into a lifestyle, and "poor me" has become an idol. Self is exalted over God. We aren't hearing His voice nor hearing His call because we are too busy listening to our own complaints and whines.

We aren't caring for others because we are too busy coddling ourselves. We are kept (and choosing to be) ineffective in God's Kingdom. There is always someone worse off, always a story worse than ours, always a situation more heartbreaking. Always.

Please don't misunderstand; there are many hurting people who need tender care. Many who need time to grieve; many who need to be gently wrapped in God's healing and love. God is a compassionate God, and we need to show that same compassion.

However, there are others who need a good shaking of the shoulders to wake up.

I've been there, done that--sat and stewed and mourned. And the longer I stewed in my stew, the stinkier my stew (and me) became. Ugh.

Christ took our sins on Himself, rose from the grave and conquered death to set us free to live free. His mercies are new every morning -- God's amazing love wrapped in forgiveness, mercy, grace, hope, and new life. God heals the brokenhearted, binds their wounds, and sets captives free.

When past issues resurface, when a memory returns, when we are sitting in our own stew, let's immediately wrap the lies of the enemy in God's truth. Allow God to get to the root and pull it out, and allow His light to shine on the darkness.

God's power isn't limited to partial, maybe, or sometimes, because nothing is impossible with God.

Hop out of the pot my friends, and walk free in the newness of life!

Heavenly Father, help me to get out of the pot of self-stewing. Thank You Father for Your freedom, never-ending hope, and new life!

~ Clean Up On Aisle Three! ~

When I was pregnant with our son, I asked the doctor what I would do if my water broke in public.

His solution?

Always carry a jar of pickles—if your water breaks, smash the jar on the floor and no one will be the wiser. Thank goodness, I never needed such a creative diversion tactic.

However when it comes to sin, it's so easy to try and divert attention away from what we've done. Adam and Eve even tried this method. Adam blamed Eve, and Eve blamed the snake, and mankind was left in a mess.

God knew we didn't need a diversion, we needed a Savior. Thankfully God demonstrated His own love for us in this: while we were still sinners, Christ died for us.

So if today you're sitting in a pickle of a mess, call for clean up. God has the absolute best method – If we confess our sins, He is faithful and just to forgive us and to clean up all our messes.

Heavenly Father thank You that no mess is too big for You. Thank You for Your forgiveness, grace, and mercy that covers all our sins.

~ Romans 5:8, 1 John 1:9

~ *Freedom!* ~

Our sweet dog loves his blanket. When tired, he fluffs it up, finds the perfect spot then sucks on it until he falls asleep. This morning Chipper found himself attached to his blanket. Somehow the rings holding his dog tags had caught on the fabric. Poor baby just stood there looking at me with pleading, big brown eyes. Fortunately the solution came easy, and once unhinged he happily trotted outside.

Chipper's bondage may have looked soft and cuddly, but in reality kept him from experiencing true freedom.

I've had the same problem. At times it almost seems easier lugging things that swath us in an uncomfortable comfort. Getting rid of bad habits, or past issues are easier when they have the consistency of a cactus.

Jesus came to set us free – not partially, but completely. Jesus said in Luke 4:18-19, He came to proclaim freedom for the prisoners and recovery of sight for the blind, to release the oppressed, to proclaim the year of the Lord's favor.

Christ saves us, then comes big time, bonus blessings –

Freedom for prisoners, no matter what has chained you.

Open eyes for the blind, no matter how sin and this world have blinded you.

Release from oppression, no matter what has held you back.

Freedom from the past, freedom to live today, and freedom to not worry about tomorrow. Woo hoo! So if the Son sets you free, you will be free indeed. ~ John 8:36.

Thank You Heavenly Father for Your freedom!

~ *Faithfulness* ~

The faithful love of the Lord never ends! His mercies never cease. Great is his faithfulness; his mercies begin afresh each morning ~ Lamentations 3:22-23 NLT.

God's mercies never cease for those how have lost loved ones.
God's mercies never cease for those whose lives have been ravaged by storms.
God's mercies never cease for those with broken hearts.
God's mercies never cease for those struggling with illness.
God's mercies never cease for those facing financial difficulties.
God's mercies never cease for those who have lost employment.
God's mercies never cease for those with sinful pasts.
God's mercies never cease for you.
Great is His faithfulness!

~ *Spiritual Cellulite* ~

With the blessings of improved health, I've returned to an exercise routine. Weight lifting, elliptical machine, and the exercise bike are whipping this body back in shape. Six pounds are gone and even nasty cellulite is being replaced with muscle tone. Yay!

The positive changes are coming through hard work and self-denial. (i.e. put down the chocolate and run!). Even my spirit needs constant attention. Spiritual cellulite is not pretty.

Spiritual workouts are essential to a healthy, growing Christian. Reading God's word, spending time in prayer and praise, Bible studies, taking captive our thoughts and focusing on God's amazing love, power, and grace, keeps our souls tuned up and tuned in.

And the neat thing is anyone (regardless of weight, age, health status, hair color, body type, foot size, social status...) can be a spiritual Hercules.

Are you up for a good soul workout?

Exercise daily in God—no spiritual flabbiness, please! Workouts in the gymnasium are useful, but a disciplined life in God is far more so, making you fit both today and forever. ~ 1 Timothy 4:8 MSG

~ Safely Tethered ~

I'll admit it, openly and with a level of shame, I've been looking at life a little pessimistically. My focus has been on a myriad of issues and difficulties, the inadequacies within myself, instead of the sufficiency and adequacy of my Heavenly Father.

I needed to rewrite a scene for one of my novels, to immerse into heavy emotions for my character. I didn't want to go back into my past and remember, examine the scars, and open the wounds. I prayed, fought, agonized, called, and e-mailed friends for help, but I knew the words were my responsibility. They could only come from God and through Him.

Still the worry remained that if I dove too deep into the memories, I wouldn't be able to return. But the truth came this morning. We are never separated from our Savior. We are always safe in His care. We can dive without fear, for He is with us. We are tethered safely to Him for eternity.

God's promises are true for all His children. No matter what you have been through, where your past has carried you, where you are right now at this moment, you will never be separated from the love of God.

For I am convinced that neither death nor life, neither angels nor demons, neither the present nor the future, nor any powers, neither height nor depth, nor anything else in all creation, will be able to separate us from the love of God that is in Christ Jesus our Lord. ~ Romans 8:38-39 NIV

~ *Drop It!* ~

The area trees were leafed in the newness of spring. However, one of our trees remained clothed in fall colors. Even though new life is showing, the tree refused to drop the leaves of the past. Many of you are going through difficulties. Some are faced with continued illness and trials.

Every day may be a challenge, however <u>every</u> day God is doing <u>new</u> things. When we hold onto the leaves of the past, the leaves won't leave us alone, and the new can't come. God never wastes a moment. His mercies are new every morning. His grace and strength are available and sufficient. Jesus didn't come to set the captives partially free, He came to set us fully free. Nothing is impossible with God. Don't look back, look up. Don't hold on, let go. Drop the old and accept the amazing, God-given new!

The Lord says, forget what happened before, and do not think about the past. Look at the new thing I am going to do. It is already happening. Don't you see it? I will make a road in the desert and rivers in the dry land. ~ Isaiah 43:18-19 NCV

~ *Is God Enough?* ~

When people turn away. When the job ends. When your family won't speak to you. When your loved one dies. When the bills are due and money is short. When the diagnosis is heart wrenching. When nothing is going right. When your world shakes. Is God enough?

Though the fig tree does not bud and there are no grapes on the vines, though the olive crop fails and the fields produce no food, though there are no sheep in the pen and no cattle in the stalls, yet I will rejoice in the Lord, I will be joyful in God my Savior ~ Habakkuk 3:17-18.

Even though I walk through the valley of the shadow of death, I will fear no evil, for you are with me; your rod and your staff, they comfort me ~ Psalm 23:4.

Though an army besiege me, my heart will not fear; though war break out against me, even then will I be confident ~ Psalm 27:3.

Though my father and mother forsake me, the LORD will receive me ~ Psalm 27:10.

Though you have made me see troubles, many and bitter, you will restore my life again; from the depths of the earth you will again bring me up ~ Psalm 71:20.

Though I walk in the midst of trouble, you preserve my life; you stretch out your hand against the anger of my foes, with your right hand you save me ~ Psalm 138:7.

Therefore we will not fear, though the earth give way and the mountains fall into the heart of the sea, though its waters roar and foam and the mountains quake with their surging ~ Psalm 46:2-3.

Though He slay me, yet will I hope in Him ~ Job 13:15.

Heavenly Father, You are always enough.

~ Sabbath Rest ~

Sunday afternoon. Church and lunch has come and gone. I gather my Bible, Bible study, and my Kindle with words waiting to be read. Small heater blowing warmth into the room, I curl into my recliner. My soul kneels at God's feet, prayers of thanksgiving echo and travel to heaven's throne.

There are so many blessings—small and large—they all speak of God's love. I don't want to slip from earth's existence to life everlasting without watching, accepting, and experiencing the gifts of His hand.

I don't want to limit His love and power. I don't want my human thoughts, ideals, and desires to stand in His way.

And so I rest.

Stilling my soul in the depth of quiet, opening my heart to hear His voice, my praise wings to His indwelt presence.

Precious Heavenly Father, may I always dwell in Your presence and love.

He who dwells in the shelter of the Most High will rest in the shadow of the Almighty. ~ Psalm 91:1 NIV

~ *Give It To God* ~

Life is not fair. I hate that statement, but it's true. Bad things happen. Life is full of emotional, physical, and spiritual hurts. Outward injuries leave scars but internal injuries carve valleys in souls. The combination of the two can be devastating. We can't fix what happened in the past, can't erase any of it. But we can take every bit to God, the Great Physician.

The fifth chapter of John relates the story of a man who had been an invalid for thirty-eight years. The man and many others—the blind, lame, and paralyzed—waited by the pool of Bethesda. This was no ordinary pool, occasionally it would be stirred by the touch of an angel, and the first one in would be healed. Day after day this man and others would watch, wait, and pray for a miracle.

And then Jesus arrives and asks, "Do you want to be made well?" For thirty-eight years this man had been waiting for healing. Yet he responds, "I can't, sir, for I have no one to put me into the pool when the water bubbles up. Someone else always gets there ahead of me." Jesus responded, "Rise, take up your bed and walk." And immediately the man was made well, took up his bed, and walked.

We cannot always choose what happened or is happening in our lives, however we do have an option how we respond. When we refuse to release our pain, infirmities, painful memories, wrongs committed against us, we become like the invalid at the pool complaining that no one is there to carry us, even as the Great Physician stands with His hand outstretched asking, "Do you want to get well?"

Freedom and healing comes when we release them to God— completely and totally. Remove the excuses, take it to Him. He is waiting.

But you don't know how bad it was or is. There is too much sorrow. Give it to God, He upholds the cause of the oppressed; He sets prisoners free He has taken account of your sorrows, all your tears in His bottle and everyone recorded in His book ~ Psalm 56:8, Psalm 146:7.

I can't forgive. I need to tell them how much they hurt me, how wrong they were. Give it to God, because if you forgive others, you will be forgiven. If you don't forgive others, you won't be forgiven. God promises to avenge and repay ~ Matthew 6:14-15, Romans 12:19.

I'm so weak and afraid. I can't do it without help. Give It to God, He gives strength to His people and blesses them with peace. Don't let your hearts be troubled and do not be afraid. You can do everything through Him who gives you strength ~ Psalm 29:11, John 14:27, Philippians 4:13.

But I need to talk about it more, I need more sympathy, I need more time, nobody understands. Give it to God, cast your cares on Him. He will sustain you; He will never let the righteous fall. He is good, a refuge in times of trouble. He cares for those who trust in Him ~ Psalm 55:22, Nahum 1:7.

Thank you Heavenly Father that You are greater than the past and greater than any trouble. You understand. You care. You have the ears, the arms, the legs, the strength, the might, the justice, the vengeance, the counsel, the comfort, the healing, the peace, the joy, and the life everlasting. I'm giving my all to You.

~ *Thankseeking* ~

I know God is always there, but part of me pulled away and I'm desperate to return to the deep-water of His presence. My heart's desire is to honor God—to bring Him glory and share of His grace, mercy, renewal, and restoration. I want to feed His sheep and tell those who are lost and hurting about God's love. I want to keep pushing through, running the race, being strong even when I'm weak.

I want to be filled to the brim with God's living water, and instead I find myself spiritually dehydrated. For too long I have been filling my spiritual bucket, sipping, and passing on God's truths and not taking time to saturate myself.

I'm parched.

I've found myself more consumed with connecting with online friends more than connecting with God. I need time to allow for body healing and soul renewal, to rest and refuel with the Lord. I'm so thankful for God and all He has done in my life. And not just for now or for a temporary time, I want to remain in a spirit of thanksgiving and thankseeking – always thanking God and forever seeking to remain in His wonderful presence.

Because in moments of thanksgiving we encounter more of God. Our eyes are lifted from our daily existence to the amazing existence of our ever-lasting, never-failing God. So to revive and renew our souls, draw deep from the living water of His word. Seek Him and you will find Him. Draw near to Him and He will draw near to You. Thank Him and seek Him and relish in the joys of Happy Thankseeking!

Heavenly Father I seek Your presence. And as I seek You I find You and Your joy. Thank You Father!

~ *Hearts Of Stone* ~

I collect rocks in the shape of hearts. I find them in streams, parking lots, in our own back yard, and wherever my journey leads. Their stone faces remind me that even in nature God speaks of His love. They are memorials of how God changed, and continues to change, my stony heart.

His grace covered my sins.
His love broke through my defensive walls.
His healing touch repaired my wounds.
His peace guards my heart through times of trouble.

How has God touched **your** heart?

I will give you a new heart and put a new spirit in you; I will remove from you your heart of stone and give you a heart of flesh. ~ Ezekiel 36:26 NIV

~ God's Sufficiency ~

There are so many hurting people, so much violence, trauma, and heartaches. Reality almost overwhelms. I want to take away world hunger and stop the wars. I want to fix everyone's problems, take away the pain and help those without Jesus find Him. I'll be honest I think I would curl into a fetal position if the solution was only through me. Fortunately during my Bible study time, I came across these verses to help me get back my prospective.

You began your life in Christ by the Spirit. Now you're trying to make it completely your own power? That's foolish. You won't succeed by your own strength or power but by My Spirit, says the Lord All-Powerful. ~ Galatians 3:3, Zechariah 4:6.

I can't do anything without God. I can't make it a moment without Him to guide me. I can't fix the world, but I can rest in The One who can. The only way I can stand firm is to remember God's truths found in His words.

He promises to search for the lost and bring back the strays. He binds up the injured and strengthens the weak. He wants all men to be saved and to come to a knowledge of the truth. ~ Ezekiel 34:16, 1 Timothy 2:3-6.

He delivers. The angel of the Lord encamps around those who fear Him, and He delivers them. He delivers from the wicked and saves His children because they take refuge in Him. He fulfills the desires of those who fear Him, He hears their cry and saves them ~ Psalm 34:7 Psalm 37:40, Psalm 145:19.

He watches and listens. Evening, morning, and noon when we cry, He hears our voice. The eyes of the Lord are on the righteous and His ears are attentive to their cry. The Lord hears and answers from His holy hill. ~ Psalm 55:17, Psalm 34:15, Psalm 3:4.

He heals the brokenhearted and binds their wounds. He forgives sins and heals all diseases. ~ Psalm 147:3. Psalm 103:2-3.

God is a refuge for the oppressed, a stronghold in times of trouble. Those who dwell in the shelter of the Most High will rest in the shadow of the Almighty. Covered with His feathers under His wings we find refuge; His faithfulness a shield and rampart. ~ Psalm 9:9, Psalm 91:1, Psalm 91:4).

God is our rest. He beckons those who are weary and burdened to come to Him and He will give rest. To take His yoke on you and learn from Him. For He is gentle and humble in heart and you will find rest for your souls. For His yoke is easy and His burden is light. Our souls find rest in God alone, our salvation comes from Him. ~ Matthew 11:28-30, Psalm 62:1.

He is our victor. He provides peace. The world brings trouble, but take heart He has overcome the world. And when we go to our eternal home with Him, He will wipe every tear from our eyes. There will be no more death or mourning or crying or pain, for the old things will pass away. Seated on His throne, he says, I am making everything new! ~ John 16:33, Revelation 21:4-5.

Heavenly Father thank You for Your unfailing promises, help me to always stand firm on the sufficiency of You.

~ *Forever In Your Heart* ~

You are the light.
You are truth.
You walk me through the past and wipe my tears.
You are healing and restoration.

Oh God, You are my everything.
Hold me close.
Never let me stray.
And forever wrap my soul tenderly in Your heart.

You hold my hand and walk me to tomorrow.
Protect me, guide me, show me Your way.
You are hope for every step.

Oh God, You are my everything.
Hold me close.
Never let me stray.
Forever wrap my soul tenderly in Your tender heart.

I am Yours.
Forever in Your heart.

~ Are You "Good" Enough For Heaven? ~

Many people think if they are "good" people they will go to heaven. However, how do you know you are good enough?

There's an old joke about two hunters in the woods being chased by a bear. One hunter yells out to the other as he runs past, "I don't have to be faster than the bear, I just have to beat you!" Unfortunately most people think the same is true about gaining entrance to heaven. Just do better than the others, be good and it will all work out fine.

The problem this presents is:

Who says how much goodness is required?

Who is keeping score?

And at any given moment, how can I know where I stand?

Does that mean as long as we are better than Adolf Hitler or Attila the Hun we've got a shot? But what if we have to be as good as a Mother Theresa or Billy Graham? Okay, maybe our chances aren't as good.

The Bible goes to the real issue with God and sets it straight for us. None of us deserves to go to Heaven, we are all sinners. His word tells us in Romans 3:23, that everyone has sinned and no one measures up to God's glory. There is no way, through our own "goodness" that we can ever stand in front of a Holy God. We tend to rank sins, but God says sin is sin.

Sometimes that doesn't sound fair. Don't all the "good" people deserve to go to Heaven? Well then again who defines fair and what makes one deserving? Hmm, okay, this is getting a little tougher.

Think about this, the designer and creator of the universe (God) also made the rules and the way for salvation. He knew we would sin, and no matter how hard we try we would never reach perfection. Yes, we can be pretty good, but our being good doesn't result in purity and holiness. With God it's not just how bad we are, it's how good we're not. Again the Bible says, "all have sinned."

So how do you know you can get into Heaven? You must have faith (absolute trust) in God and His way to heaven. And He didn't make it difficult–not for us anyway.

Jesus, His only Son (God in the flesh), willingly sacrificed His life through dying on the cross to make the way clear for us to get to our heavenly home. Jesus was/is the sacrifice for our sins. Three days after His death, He rose again.

And because Jesus triumphed over death, hell, and the grave, He held the keys to eternal life. He said Himself that He is the way, the truth and the life and that no one comes to the Father except through Him ~John 14:6. Peter, one of His closest followers said that salvation is only found in Jesus and there is no other name under heaven by which we are saved ~ Acts 4:12.

Only through Jesus' death for us can the door be opened–the invitation extended for every man, woman, and child. He did something for us that we could not do for ourselves. He bridged the gap between us and a Holy Father ... Jesus became God's way.

From the cross, Jesus finished the work His Father sent Him to do, by dying for the liar, the gossip, the profane, murderer, thief, abuser, drunkard, and adulterer–every sinner. He died for you and for me. And when He died, He said, "It is finished."

We cannot measure up, but we can give up, and when we do, the cross bridges the gap, the door is opened, and we can stand clothed in the Holy righteousness of Jesus Christ. He is the door and everyone who enters through Him will be saved ~ John 10:9. Are you ready to give up on your preconceived ideas about the way to heaven? If "yes" then let's stop thinking about the "goodness trap," it's not an issue ... so what is the next step?

Jesus said He stands at the door knocking, waiting for us to hear Him, open the door to Him ~ Revelation 3:20. The door is open and your goodness isn't the issue. Once you repent of your sins and ask Him to be your Lord and Savior, He works in you to help and free you from the bondages of sin.

Sin promises fun but only results in bondage. Christ offers freedom. He is the "get out of hell for free card."

Why is it so easy? Because God is good, God is love, and God wants nothing more than for you to come home to the Heaven He created for His beautiful but marred creation.

Good works, church membership, denominations, religiosity, good family history, etc. won't get you into Heaven. Even saying you believe in God isn't enough. The Bible says, the even the demons believe in God and they shudder ~ James 2:19.

Receiving salvation means desiring a personal relationship with Jesus Christ. So what do you do? The apostle Paul put it pretty plainly that if you confess with your mouth that Jesus is Lord and believe in your heart that God raised Him from the dead, you will be saved ~ Romans 10:9-10.

Will you pray this simple prayer acknowledging Jesus' death for your salvation?

"Lord Jesus, I'm the sinner you came to save and I need You. Thank You for dying on the cross for my sins. I open the door of my life and receive You as my Savior and Lord. Thank You for forgiving my sins and giving me eternal life. Please take control of my life and make me the kind of person You want me to be." In Jesus' Name, Amen!

Now there, you've done it ... it wasn't difficult was it? There weren't a long list of things you had to do before you can be forgiven. It was all done for you. That's what we call grace—God giving us something we need but don't deserve. And now that you belong to Him, He wants to live His life though you. The God who made you, loves you more than anyone ever could or will, wants the world to see His Son living in you. Sounds like a great deal to me!

Okay, so if you have done this, does that mean your whole life will change? You betcha! And here's what you should expect. Your new life is being changed from the inside out. A personal relationship with Jesus Christ is a spark that cannot be extinguished, a safe harbor in the storms of life, hope and peace that never ends, joy midst sorrow, and life everlasting.

What's next? Find a good Bible-teaching church and when you feel it's time, talk to your pastor about being baptized. Begin to share with others what has taken place in your life. And never start and end the day without taking time to pray (talking with God). He does exist and He wants to begin to work on your behalf.

So now you're fit for Heaven and believe me, it won't be a place where we sit around with little angel wings bored to tears playing harps. It is a vibrant, exciting, peaceful, ecstatic place of fellowship, love, and never ending joy.

If you prayed that prayer, *welcome home* to your eternal home!

~ *Closing Prayer* ~

Heavenly Father I want to go to the depths of Your love and wisdom to attain all the depths of Your knowledge my finite brain can contain. I want to live fully the life You've given me. I want to only desire that which You desire and live as You want me to live. Your judgments and Your ways are unfathomable. For from You and through You all things exist. I present me to You. I lay across Your altar, my mind, body, heart, strength, and soul. I sacrifice to You my will to align fully with Yours. I throw off everything and anything that hinders, entangles, and keeps me from running free the race You have given for me to run. Purify and refine me so all may see through me, straight to You.

Thank You for giving me life. Thank You for loving me even when I am so unlovely. Thank You for granting me grace when I am so unworthy. Thank You for Your mercy when I don't deserve mercy. Thank You that You always want to hear my voice, and no concern is too small or too big. Thank You for allowing me to cry on Your shoulder and to laugh and play without condemnation. Thank You for always being available, never turning me away, and always waiting with open arms. Thank You for Your freely offered peace and joy. Thank You for Your loving, eternal care. Thank You for welcoming home the prodigal children. Thank You for Your family around the world of every race and creed. Heavenly Father, thank You that Your love is love enough for us all. I love You,

I fix my eyes on You, Jesus. I long to live, joyfully, free. Abba Daddy, my heart is forever Yours.

~ About The Author ~

Lisa Buffaloe is a writer, speaker, happily-married mom, founder and host for Living Joyfully Free Radio. Lisa's past experiences—molestation by a baby-sitter, assault, rape by a doctor, divorce, being stalked, cancer, death of loved ones, multiple surgeries, and eleven years of chronic illness from Lyme Disease—bless her with a backdrop to share God's amazing love, healing, and restoration. Regardless of our past, through Jesus Christ we truly can live joyfully free.

Novels by Lisa Buffaloe
Nadia's Hope
Prodigal Nights
Grace for the Char-Baked (Novella)

Visit Lisa at these sites…
www.LisaBuffaloe.com
www.livingjoyfullyfree.com
www.Twitter.com/lisabuffaloe
www.Facebook.com/lisabuffaloe
www.fliterary.com (Fun for the Literary)
www.twitter.com/livingjoyfullyf
www.twitter.com/fliterary

Made in the USA
Charleston, SC
27 April 2013